Loving Dylan

J. MARIE

PAGE PUBLISHING, INC.
Conneaut Lake, PA

First originally published by Page Publishing 2020

ISBN 978-1-64584-216-3 (pbk)
ISBN 978-1-64584-217-0 (digital)

Printed in the United States of America

Dear Reader,

Originally, this was started as my fourth step; I was trying to find my part. Then it turned into a letter to my son in order that he might understand that I deeply love him and the actions I took only served this love. It occurred to me that he is not as interested in my point of view as you might be. To be clear, I still don't know what I am doing. This project started in earnest during lunch with four women, three of us have sons that are chronic drug users. All of us were feeling inadequate for the task at hand and confused by our situation.

The question is, how did I get here? I tried so hard. I read every parenting magazine and paid top real estate prices for the right neighborhood and, more importantly, the right schools. Our family went to church every Sunday and ate dinner as a family on most nights. My hope is that by sharing my experience, strength, and hope, you find your power.

Our family uses four-letter words, including the word *love*, but I will not offend you with unnecessary profanity; except when the words are part of the storyline. So when you read the words *golly gee whiz* or *heck*, please understand that these are the least offensive version of heated discussions. Take comfort, though, this has a happy ending. This is less about the ending and more about the journey getting there. Thank you for taking this journey with me.

The Word of God on Fire

Why would loving parents drug their son to drive him across state lines so that he could be held hostage by people they had never met? It was March 16, 2011. I woke up at 4:30 a.m. to start work so that I could go to school with my oldest son, Dylan. It generally took three hours to go over his homework and get his new assignments. I had to make the work day up on the front end; there was a general sense of fatigue at all times. I was at my desk when Dylan told me he was leaving the house and would be back in a few hours. We were due at the high school in one hour, so I was trying to finish the appraisal report due that day before we left.

This started an argument because he had already missed two sessions, and he was going to be kicked out of the home school program if he missed another week. His teacher was nice, but not a pushover. Dylan and I were yelling loudly at each other when Craig interrupted us. Dylan was insisting that he had to leave to pay people off and that if he didn't he would be hurt.

Part of my brain was amused that he was making the wrong argument. What was I supposed to say to the school when I called in his absence? "Sorry my kid missed school today. He had to finish his drug dealing so that people won't hurt him." We were both frantic and loud when, Dylan's father and my husband, Craig walked into the argument and tried to separate us. Craig's method was consistent. He typically chose the one that he felt was not in their reptilian brain. In this instance, it was me. He felt like I was the one that could be reasoned with.

His form of reasoning was to argue the other's point in a calm voice. He started with shame by telling me that I need to "act like an adult." Of course, to prove him wrong, I calmed down immediately; his methods were effective momentarily. Dylan looked victorious as Craig was explaining to me that we could excuse the absence and reschedule the class. I would not be surprised if my head exploded at this point. The assumption that I didn't think of the obvious infuriated me. In my thinking, Craig thought I was one of two things. The first that I am stupid and can't solve a simple problem, and the other is that I am a control freak and picking a fight with Dylan to prove a point.

After explaining to Craig that the reality is that we could not do that because we had already done that for the last two weeks. Like a broken record, I spelled out that we were in danger of losing his spot in the program and didn't have a pocketful of options. It is not like the teacher has a whole classroom. The class was a one-on-one session.

I lost my temper and started yelling when Craig said that we would just find a new school and Dylan announced, "I told you she's a crazy bitch." My hysteria was crazy looking. I was angry that I had worked so hard with no result, and I hated being in this triangle of two against one. The more I tried, the more Dylan pushed back. He was using the words *cunt*, *bitch*, and, weirdly, *slut* at me regularly. I didn't understand the word *slut* because I had never cheated on Craig. I never even gave the impression of impropriety. It was a point with me because Craig has his own set of insecurities with our twenty-year age difference, and I dated people I had no business dating in my drinking days. Craig's insecurities were deepened with his diagnosis of Parkinson's four years prior. I understood *crazy* and *bitch* because I was fierce in my determination.

Craig must have been as exhausted as I was because he grabbed Dylan by the shirt and told him he was leaving the house today for the school in Nevada. He went to the hall closet where we kept the bag packed with the items the school listed for admission. I didn't know what Craig's plan was to get him to the school. The school was eleven hours away, and I don't drive because I have a vision impairment that prohibits me from driving. Driving him by himself seemed dangerous; we couldn't even be in the same office without an altercation.

Dylan had removed my Bible from the bag. It was the only Bible in the house, given to me in a moment of despair in my youth. I was in the office calling 911 when he turned the gas stove on and caught the Bible on fire. The dispatcher had trouble understanding me as I was describing the events in the household. She repeatedly told me to calm down, but I couldn't. The wall of containment I had built over the last year to keep myself upright and functioning crumbled. The fear and sorrow overwhelmed me. I was worried that one of us would not live through this experience. My anger with Craig was replaced with pity. He was shaking uncontrollably when the police arrived.

The house was filled with smoke, but the Bible was in the kitchen sink, soaked in water. The fire truck left once they figured out they weren't needed. The ambulance was parked in the driveway, and the two police cars were blocking the road. Betty and Virgil, our neighbors across the street, were standing on their fresh-mowed lawn in their slippers, talking to their neighbor who had sat in their lawn chairs to watch the action. All we could do was wave and cheerfully yell, "Everything's okay. No worries." I asked the officers if they could turn the lights off so we didn't attract even more neighbors.

Officer Cooper was so calm. He sent Dylan out to talk to the other police officers who emptied his pockets and listened to his side of the story with great interest and compassion. As Dylan was leaving in an ambulance to be held for seventy-two hours in a psychiatric hold, I went back to the office to make sure we had a bed in the school in Nevada. I asked Craig to lie down so he could rest before his trip, but he was too stimulated to lie down. He made me a cup of coffee instead.

With the cup of coffee, he hugged me. "I am sorry for losing control." I stopped my phone calls to accept his apology and issue my own.

"I am sorry too. This is a crazy situation. There's no rule book in how to deal with this crap. What do you do when your flesh and blood acts like that?" I had to control my voice when I answered the phone. "Appraisals."

Between phone calls, we continued the conversation, "I thought things were going to be so different. I would be a dead person if I spoke to my parents like that. There would be an imprint on the wall of my face."

He seemed relieved we were talking. "I know. My dad never hit me, but I knew the danger was there, and I never wanted to see it."

The hospital wanted Dylan to go home within an hour of arrival. They didn't have a bed for a teenage boy on the adult psychiatric unit, and the teen unit is in the next county. I told them we were not picking him up right away, and they would have to hold him there for a few more hours while I arranged for transport to Nevada. The big goons that professionally transport charge $2,000 that I didn't have. Our friend Scott, a retired probation officer, called Rick, and they agreed to drive the eleven hours, each way, to transport Dylan with Craig. Rick even used his car.

When Craig picked Dylan up with Scott and Rick, he gave Dylan two prescription sleeping pills even though it was three in the afternoon. He could sleep through California. I didn't go to the hospital. I stayed behind to shower and wash the chaos off so I could pick up our youngest son, Robbie, from school. Robbie cried when I told him that Dylan would be living in Nevada for a while. Just before we walked in the front door, he slipped his hand in mine and told me, "It's okay, Mom. I love you." I needed to hear that right at that moment.

According to the blow-by-blow reporting during the drive, Dylan vacillated between anger and fear. He was so angry that he was swearing at all the grown men in the car and, at one point, sprayed root beer all over the car. I hate being sticky, so I am glad I wasn't there. Just before crossing into Nevada, Craig called and told me that Dylan promised that he would behave if he was given another chance. Dylan was crying on the phone while begging me to reconsider. He promised he would go to school and never do drugs. He told me how much he loved me and that he was sorry that he had called me terrible names.

I had already prepared myself for this moment. When I told him no, he called me a bitch and hung up the phone. I was actually grateful for the *bitch* word because it confirmed my response. I knew that I might not get another opportunity. Rick and Scott weren't ever going to come back again. I knew that Dylan's promises were instantly well intended, but he would be back to the behavior within a few days. This was a familiar dance. I needed to think about our family as a whole.

Dylan was brave going into the school. He told his dad he loved him and gave him a hug. Craig cried for several hundred miles going home. I was angry when he called crying because I wondered if we would be in this situation if he was less involved in poker and more involved in the family. He wouldn't even regularly attend the STEP classes that I had arranged to be taught at our church. STEP stands for Systematic Training for Effective Parenting. I was angry that now he cries; I had cried for the previous year. I had asked the men to stay in a hotel, but Craig had to get back to a fundraiser poker tournament, so they drove the entire trip, stopping only for gas and snacks.

Two Priests and Two Therapists

Our journey started on a sunny April day in Dylan's 8th grade year. I didn't mean to slam the car door; my legs were simply eager to climb the hill. They were digging through every step with the muscle memory of the twice a week for the past six months. As I stood at the top, looking at the valley spread before me, I hoped to get a minute to calm down before Craig arrived. He was ten minutes behind me, which isn't bad for an old man with Parkinson's disease. His silly dog was trying to keep up with him with her short little legs.

"Sorry, I didn't mean to slam the door." The front of his shirt was wet with sweat. "Can we start over?"

"Sure." His voice was still curt, but the fact that he was standing there said everything. "What do you think we should do?"

"I don't know. What did your parents do?" This seemed a reasonable start. I waited with irritation for him to catch his breath.

"They didn't know until the night my mom found me in the front yard. She screamed because she thought I was dead. I was just drunk and passed out." He was still panting. "I was already married with a pregnant wife, so what were they going to do?" Lily, the Cavalier King Charles

11

spaniel he paid too much money for, finally arrived. "What did your parents do?"

"Are you kidding?" I was trying to regulate my tone. "My stepmom beat the heck out of me when she found my birth control pills. I was seventeen years old, but the next year, she would hand me a garbage bag and tell me that I was old enough to start paying my own rent. There was no way I was going to get caught drinking. They had no idea."

"What do you think we should do?" he asked again. I could feel the anger rising again.

"I don't know. They changed the parenting rules. You can't beat them anymore or even hurt their feelings." Now I was just venting, but he was getting charged out of this familiar tangent.

"What did Bruce and Stephen say?" He was referring to the phone call to our priests an hour earlier.

"They said not to overreact. It's perfectly normal, and they gave the stats of kids that try drugs and alcohol in their youth, but I can't remember the stats. I was too busy spinning out." He was bent over giving Lily water. "They told me not to overreact three times. It kind of hurt my feelings, like I am always overreacting."

"No, you never overreact." His sarcasm landed appropriately. We were both laughing.

Before we left for our hike, it was a typical Friday morning, cleaning for the cleaning ladies. Craig was stripping Dylan's bed to put clean sheets on when he found a marijuana pipe and a stash of marijuana under the twin mattress. My brain short-circuited. There were too many thoughts in my head at one time. The first was that Craig is very thorough when he does help clean the house; I would have never found that. Secondly, Dylan is just fourteen and we are starting this already. Of course, my recovering alcoholic/drug addict brain goes to my young son shooting up in an alley and living under a bridge. Third, I wondered where he got this weed. It smelled powerful with the little purple hairs; I never got weed like that.

Together, Craig and I freaked out and blamed each other. The only reason to have a spouse is to have someone to blame everything on. It can't be my fault because I watched him like a hawk. Dylan wasn't even allowed to go downtown unsupervised and had to come directly home from school. I knew where he was at every moment like all good helicopter moms. I even ran our appraisal business from home so I could be there when our three kids came home from school. I made sure the kids were properly educated with supplementary music and art classes when the public schools stopped teaching these in school.

I knew the kids' friends and their parents. We had lived in the same home for twelve years and even did an addition to the home so that we didn't have to move out of the neighborhood. We wanted our three kids, Dylan, Claire, and Robbie, to have a stable life in a safe neighborhood. The neighborhood was a mid-century housing tract with a tiny well-run elementary school where the principal knew every student and their circle of friends. Definitely "leave it to beaver" land except that I was not June Cleaver and Craig was definitely not Ward. We both swear like sailors, and I don't own any pearls or high heels.

We were living in San Francisco when I got pregnant and knew we didn't want to raise our child in San Francisco. It was difficult leaving our one-bedroom apartment which was across the street from the rose garden in Golden Gate Park. There were three museums and an aquarium within walking distance; more with a bus ride. The new home lacked the charm of the Victorian flat, but we chose Martinez because we thought we might be insulated from this very day. Craig and I are both recovering alcoholic and drug addicts with a rich history of naked escapades. Some of our tales are humorous, but mostly pathetic. Of course, both of us went to the end of our own stories with Dylan.

When we came to our senses, we did what every rational parent does when they find their fourteen-year-old son's weed. We called our two priests. Both are married with kids; we are Episcopalians. They are not married to each other although they could in our tradition. Bruce is married with older children, and Stephen is married with young children. Both are wonderful men with a healthy understanding of our histories. After they talked us off the ledge, they gave us the number of a family therapist. They also reminded us that although we should be concerned, we should not future jump.

As we hung up the phone, it occurred to us that we were grateful we had deeply rooted ourselves into the church. We were not particularly religious but felt we needed a local support system. Our families are scattered across the United States. Craig had come from a Catholic tradition, and I had grown up Missouri Synod Lutheran. Except for the hellfire and brimstone from the pulpit, it was helpful being raised in a group of people focused on service in the world. I wanted something similar for my family but without the judgement. When I met Bruce outside the pre-school, located on the church campus, he cracked a joke, and I thought I could go to a church with a funny priest.

After a lengthy interview with Bruce regarding the dogma and teachings of the Episcopal Church, we started regularly attending services. I am not sure that after our interview Bruce wanted us to go to the church. My questions were more concerned with who's in and who's out. It was important to me that the church is not just tolerant of all people no matter who they love, but I wanted a church that was affirming. Tolerate is a hateful word.

Craig almost got us kicked out before we even officially joined. With a straight face and no warning, he asked Bruce, wearing his priest collar, "How do you feel about masturbation?" I wondered what Bruce would think if I either fell through the floor or punched my husband in the face. Bruce's face froze in the way that I now know means "don't react."

He asked with bemusement, "Why do you ask?"

"I want to know what you are going to be teaching my kids about sex." Both Bruce and I let out a sigh. This was a reasonable question. A warning would have helped.

Without missing a beat, Bruce replied, "It's a personal matter, don't you think?"

By the time Dylan got home from school, we were calmer and had a plan in place. If he had walked in even thirty minutes earlier, he would have witnessed our craziness up close and personal instead of the watered-down version. He knew he was in trouble when we were sitting in the living room when he got home instead of at our desks. The color drained from his face when his dad said his name.

"Dylan, your mom and I found your pipe and your weed." This was a good start. His voice was firm, but loving. "We need to know if you are in trouble." Good job, Craig.

"No. That is not mine." We expected this response. "I am keeping it for my friend because he has abusive parents. I knew that if you found me with it you would be reasonable." Nice touch.

"So you don't mind taking this test?" I pulled out a marijuana drug test; my self-satisfaction was not missed by Dylan.

"Are you proud of yourself, Mom? Let me guess, you knew I would say that." He knew me too well. One of drawbacks of spending so much time with my kids is that they also know me and my foils.

"A little." I was shrinking into myself.

"Okay. I smoked a little," he continued. "I am holding it for a friend, but I did try it and I didn't like it. I am never doing it again."

Craig was tired of the Dylan/Mom dance and walked away, saying, "We have an appointment after school tomorrow with a therapist. Don't be late or you are on restriction."

The first therapist was a disabled man with MS who could not walk independently. I wondered if this was a good fit for my son who was, at the moment, image driven. He had stopped doing all the things that would be seen as not cool. The *Lord of the Rings* trilogy was now his shameful secret. Now it was all about the SKA music and the right hair and clothes. I forced him to go to the therapy meetings, which were both family and private sessions. The therapist was expensive but came highly recommended by Colin and his father.

Colin, a new friend, was unlike any friend Dylan had ever had. He was masculine and loved showing his physique with wifebeater T-shirts. He could barely read and was hyperactive. His family, a gay single dad and older brother, went to our church. I was conflicted; Colin was loyal and funny but also the troublemaker of the church, but at least he was associated with a faith community. These two boys were so different that I wondered what they talked about. I was pretty sure they weren't reading scripture.

At a cost of 150 per hour, the therapist told us all the ways that we were failing as parents in front of Dylan. Dylan loved him. He couldn't wait to go to the family sessions. The private sessions seemed to be going well too. Dylan called him Yoda because he had the same cadence and sentence structure as Yoda from the *Star Wars* movie. The therapist seemed to think he was making progress with three sessions a week, and there were a few weeks with negative drug tests. He did inform us that Dylan had psychological issues that are concerning. Of course, he would not tell us what Dylan was saying in the individual sessions that would lead him to believe we are in for a world of hurt. There are patient privacy laws.

We just kept paying, and he just kept telling us that Dylan should spend more time with Colin because Colin was good boy. One day, while at church, Colin's dad offered me a ride to the shopping mall Sears where the two boys were being held for theft. Of course, the boys had a story which I half believed. They reported they were simply looking at the sunglasses, and the security guard thought Colin had taken the tag off a pair and started wearing them. Colin insisted he had bought them on a different day and just happened to be looking for another pair. Dylan was wearing one of Colin's wifebeater T-shirt, which was too big for him, and a loose cotton shirt over it. I had to look again when I walked into the small security office. Dylan was slumped in the chair with his leg out and sunglasses on his head. He looked so different I was speechless for a minute.

The summer between his eighth-grade year and high school was the calm before the storm. I say that, and yet there was a lot of yelling. The parents of his old friends wouldn't let their son's hang out with him anymore, and I wouldn't allow Dylan to see his new friends anymore. There was also conflict about the decision we made to send him to a public school instead of the $14,000-a-year private boy's high school as planned. Our finances, like many in our industry, were unstable because the United States financial market was still melting in the great recession.

Therapy became too expensive, and Dylan stopped showing up on time for the sessions. He was regularly drunk and testing positive for THC. The financial crisis had hit our business with particular cruelty. Being appraisers meant that we had changes in the legislation with the Frank/Dodd Act. We made less money and had been financially bleeding for two years. Most of our staff had been laid off, and Craig, who had been diagnosed with Parkinson's disease three years prior, had to go back to work. We moved Uncle Danny in so that we could still employ him at a cut rate in exchange for rent. He now lived in my beautiful guest bedroom.

I knew Dylan had worked hard to keep his grades up so that he could qualify for the private school. Craig and I had argued about whether to send him there. All I could see was the pile of debt. The mortgage was already overwhelming, the IRS debt was inconceivable, and we still didn't have gutters on the house. It seemed irresponsible to take on more debt. Craig's argument that Dylan had worked hard for this and the expense would be negligible was a legitimate argument. I worried that Dylan would be the kid in school who had to stay in town during spring break while his classmates were skiing in Canada. This could make his struggling self-esteem sink lower. Even as I write this, I still don't know who was right.

During one of our heated discussion in which Craig bounced back and forth between Dylan's point of view and my point of view, CNN informed us that Countrywide was going bankrupt and purchased by Bank of America. I had to stop our discussion and listen to Henry Paulson, one of the architects of the American financial recovery, give the details.

"Mom, could you just finish this?" His irritation was understandable. He was making progress in the argument.

"No. Countrywide owes me $12,500 that I am probably not going to get." Like a deflated balloon, I walked out of the room to take a hot bath.

It was the tipping point of our lives, and yet it was impossible to know at the time. We found another therapist to help Dylan deal with the anger and disappointment. We still could not afford the appointments, but it was cheaper than the $14,000-a-year tuition. This therapist also spent a lot of time trying to get Craig and me on the same page. I was an anger ball, and Craig was checked out. The more Craig checked out, the louder I screamed, as though he couldn't hear me.

Years later, Dylan told me that he was telling the therapist he called "Yoda" that he was biting the heads off Pigeons. I was going broke with my smart-ass son trolling this man. I saw him at Colin's funeral three years later. Colin had died of a drug overdose in a hotel room in Tahoe. I wondered if I should tell the therapist the truth. He had been outsmarted by a fourteen-year-old kid. I decided against it. Seeing Colin's dad, Matt, at the funeral was a cluster of emotions—gratitude that I still had Dylan and guilt that I felt envious that Matt knew the end of his story—and I was still waiting to see the final outcome.

I read an article one time about the dangers of being tossed overboard into the ocean. The danger is that if you are deep enough that you cannot see the daylight on the surface, you could become disoriented and swim even farther away from the surface without realizing you are swimming fervently in the wrong direction.

I Am Not Afraid to Kill a Cowboy

I knew we were in trouble during the All in One Day at the large high school. We were there to check Dylan into school and get his class schedule. The high school has a total of 2,000 +/- students. Only the freshman and seniors were getting their class schedules. The senior boys looked like men, and Dylan was just five feet, four inches with a baby face. His shoulder never left my shoulder. His insecurity was in full bloom and evidenced by his insults. "My clothes were not in style, and the sunspots on my face should be covered with makeup. I looked like a hippie. My hair was too long, and I needed to dye my gray hair." His friend Kyle's mom was standing behind us in line with her leopard-print pants, strappy heels, and blue eye shadow. He tapped into my own insecurities with questions like, "Why couldn't you just be more like other moms?"

The first few days of high school were rough; his geometry class was harder than he expected. He had always skated through school with minimal effort because he has a good memory and was determined to be smarter than the average bear by various teachers and a psychologist. We thought, however, that he had overcome his concerns because he was up and ready for school early and left home with a smile. He had a cute girlfriend and lots of new friends. His friends were well-dressed with collared shirts. He always had a lot of girls hanging around. His marijuana drug tests were negative, so we thought we were home free and that he had overcome his bump in the road.

Craig and I were staying home on weekend nights, giving up our season tickets at the theatre so that we could better keep an eye on our kids. Having Uncle Danny in the home meant that we had another set of adult eyes. We were regularly having dinner on the table for the kids and their friends on the weekend nights so we could know them better. Dylan had some freedom given back because the drug tests were coming up negative and his friends were nice enough. They weren't the same kind of friends. They had never even heard of *Lord of the Rings* or the History channel. They were popular and the girls showed a lot of skin and their makeup was applied with a heavy hand, but they used their manners and I had never seen Dylan happier.

Our first experience with the police was a regular Friday night. I was still doing the dishes when Uncle Danny came in with his cell phone and Dylan on the other end. The police had him and his friends stopped at city hall, waiting for their parents. We raced downtown with panic where I met Kyle's mother and little brother. Dylan was against the wall with four boys. I was stunned by Dylan's attitude toward the police officer.

"Dylan, what's going on?" I focused on slowing down my breathing. Craig was behind me, meeting Kyle's mother.

"Nothing. This cop stopped us for nothing." His bravado was unfamiliar to me. Does he act like this in front of his friends? "We were just hanging out here, minding our own business."

"Why are you talking like this to the police?" We were standing in front of the city hall where I served as a commissioner for our city. I knew the police officer to be reasonable.

"Why is he stopping us for nothing?" He was not handcuffed, but he would be shortly if he didn't shut his mouth. Without thinking, I smacked him at the back of his head and told him to apologize and shut up.

After he had apologized, Officer Gartner told him, "You don't know how lucky you are to have your mom." The boys had been stopped for underage smoking.

The THC drug test was negative and his breathalyzer blew 0.00. He had stated that he was holding the cigarettes for someone else, but when I asked him to empty his pockets at home, there was another pack of cigarettes. His confession that he was smoking cigarettes but that was all he was doing seemed sincere. I reminded him that we don't smoke inside the home. Uncle Danny was a chain-smoker. I didn't think smoking cigarettes was the end of the world at fifteen years old. It wasn't preferred, but I was happy that's all it was.

That incident made me think that maybe providing a safe place for the kids to hang out in our home on Friday nights would be better. I made sure the home was clean and loaded with junk food. Our backyard had a pool and trampoline. Our family room was huge with lots of couch space, blankets, and a large-screen TV with video games attached to the TV. Virtually, a teen paradise. It felt like a reasonable solution. We were busy congratulating ourselves when Dylan came into the home office flanked by under-dressed giggling girls.

He was sucking on a pacifier and telling us, "You guys are the best parents. Thank you so much for letting us hang out here. I love you so much." I thought the pacifier was weird, but I was overwhelmed by his words. I still had the tears of joy in my eyes when Craig had told me to come over to his computer.

He googled teenagers and pacifiers and the word *Extacy* popped up. My stomach dropped while I read the Urban Dictionary explanation. Extacy sounded fun! It floods the body with dopamine and makes the whole world feel luscious. How was I going to convince my son that geometry was more important than this drug? Apparently, the user can't stop touching things. It wasn't surprising when I found our son on the trampoline with the least dressed of the two girls in a compromising position. Later, the same girl was upstairs in Dylan's room with his best friend, Travis. The drug test was positive for MMDA, the active ingredient. The drug tests that he had been passing were too limited in scope. We needed to broaden our search.

Because Extacy is odorless, comes in a pill form, and cheap, it is hard to regulate as a parent. The test is expensive and the half-life is short for the drug—less than forty-eight hours. Marijuana has a long half-life and shows in the system for weeks. Marijuana is also expensive. Dylan was apologetic with promises to never do it again. He told us that he didn't even like it that much. The pacifiers keep the users from grinding their teeth. There's an amphetamine component to the drug. Part of my brain was grateful he was protecting the teeth we had spent $8,000 straightening with braces.

We kept randomly testing and he kept testing positive, and we kept disconnecting his phone and keeping him on restriction. The arguments were frequent and volatile. Things were slipping out of control quickly with holes in walls and doors. Craig had gone into Dylan's room after one of the arguments in which Dylan was physically threatening to me.

I was standing outside the door, cleaning up the desk in the nook, when there was a loud bang and Craig was yelling at him, "You think you can take me. Just try."

Dylan was sobbing, but I couldn't get in the door because they were fighting in front of the door. The physical altercation between Craig and Dylan happened in a flash. Dylan had pulled a knife on Craig. It was over within thirty seconds with Dylan crying in Craig's arms. They both walked away with I'm sorrys and a hug. I was shaking and scared; this was too familiar to me. This was too akin to the violence in my childhood for me to be comfortable.

We were afraid to sleep at night. We had locks on our bedroom, but it turns out it is illegal in California to lock a child in their room at night even if they have a bathroom with a sink with water and they have food. We could, as parents, be charged with unlawfully detaining a minor. When confronted by the police for this, I invited them to take him into foster care. It was my opinion that this is my child and I had a right to keep him safe, even from himself. He was sneaking out at night. If he was put in foster care, our family would be charged $3,200 per month because we had resources.

Craig's older daughter, Sheila, who was a year younger than me, had generously offered to let Dylan live with her family in Michigan. This offer was incredibly generous as she was watching Craig give another family what she always wanted. Sheila and her sister grew up in Craig's first family before Craig got sober and had been an absentee parent. I thought that marrying someone who had already had a family would be advantageous and compensate for my insecurities about motherhood. My childhood was not ideal with random acts of violence and a steady stream of neglect. Craig's advantage was that he had a happy childhood, but his guilt over his first family could impede his best instincts.

Sheila was married to Carl, an aggressive redneck who was not limited by liberal California laws. Before I had children, I bought into the new way of raising children hook, line and sinker. I thought children needed to be listened to and given every opportunity to express their feelings. I thought Carl was a caveman in his child-rearing. Maybe I was wrong. Maybe Carl had the right approach. Maybe children needed to simply do what they are told, and when they grow up, they can express their feelings in the home where they pay the rent.

When this option was presented to Dylan, he rebuked the idea. "You guys are overreacting. You are just too old-fashioned. This is normal."

I was upstairs in his room, looking out the window. "Maybe we are old-fashioned, but I think you are going overboard. We think that maybe with a fresh start with sister Sheila, you would be able to catch up in school." The tree was naked and the leaves would need raking. I thought about asking him to rake the leaves but continued, "We don't want you to stay forever, but maybe you need a break from us."

He wasn't buying my explanation. "You are sending me there, hoping that Carl will straighten me out." This blond-haired, blue-eyed boy that didn't weigh one hundred pounds soaking wet told me, "Go ahead and send me there. I'll kill Carl. I am not afraid to kill a cowboy."

I wanted to laugh, but I was too scared. It occurred to me that he really had no idea the trouble he was making for himself. His magical thinking could wind up killing him or landing him in prison. It didn't matter anyway. Sheila's offer had been rescinded when reason prevailed; she didn't need the problem either.

Man on Fire

It was a Friday night in November. I had asked for his first progress report but had gotten a lame excuse and a very sincere apology. He is the best apologizer, taking responsibility with contrition. "I learned my lesson, and it won't happen again." His friend Travis had dinner with us. I liked Travis; he had good manners and always wore a polo shirt. He was clean-cut with braces, and of course, I knew his mom.

I thought the two might be a little unnaturally happy but thought maybe it's because it was the Friday before Thanksgiving break. I was heading back into my office, after dinner, to finish an appraisal report. Working seven days a week was the norm; I worked every moment I could with gratitude to have the work. A lot of my friends who lost their jobs in the recession had more education than me. A flash of light coming from the backyard caught my attention. The porch light was on, but the only light on the lawn area was Travis rolling around the lawn, trying to put the fire out on his pant legs.

Dylan was laughing uncontrollably as Craig was squirting Travis with the hose. As the boys were trembling, sitting on the couch, dripping water, they preceded to spill the details of catching their progress reports on fire. In an attempt to hide their failing grades, they were going to burn them. Of course, because they were high on marijuana, they spilled gasoline all over their clothing while dousing their progress reports. When they lit the match, the fire was out of control in an instant.

Then I asked, "How did you think you were going to hide your grades when your report cards are mailed to the house?"

Dylan shrugged his shoulders and said, "I don't know. I didn't think of that."

"Did you get all failing grades?" I was trying to grab something real. "Can you make up any of the work?"

"Yes, Mom." They all looked at me with irritation. "Travis almost died, and you are focused on my grades?"

"Well, yes," I continued. "He didn't die, and this incident will go unremembered four years from now, but your grades are going to limit your future."

I gave him the warning that if he couldn't get credit in even one of his classes, I would pull him out of school and homeschool him. Apparently, he was walking into the front of the school when dropped off and walking right out the back door. I was a little suspicious when he was suddenly eager to get to school on time. He was in the office every day with Vice Principal Mr. Aloo, but I had no idea because Mr. Aloo was calling a dead number.

When I finally met Mr. Aloo, I was yelling at Dylan in the dean's office. Mr. Aloo stopped me with his lilting South African accent, saying, "Instead of you looking at this like Dylan is a bad boy, why don't you look at this like he has a problem that you will face together?"

I looked at him like he had rocks in his head. He must not understand the shame and disappointment that comes with having a juvenile delinquent for a son. He must not have seen the neighbor's faces when they confronted me the previous summer when Dylan was playing airsoft guns in the front yard and shot up their cars with the plastic pellets. He must not have ever gotten a phone call when, at a house christening, telling me that I better come home before the police are called. He must not have had to listen to his best friend's mother, who won't let the two boys hang out anymore together, talk about her son playing the oboe in the San Francisco youth orchestra. He must not have to explain why Dylan didn't go on the youth mission trip to the reservation in South Dakota even though we paid for the plane ticket already. He must not have to set the home alarm system every night to make sure the people in the home stay in the home. He must not have to hide the medications in the safe. If he did, he wouldn't say something so stupid.

On the verge of tears but trying to contain myself, I replied, "I'll take that into consideration, but what does he need to do to make up the semester he lost?"

Well, if we were talking about something else besides my son's future and lack thereof, I could have listened to him talk all day. His accent made even ordinary words sound like they were dipped in honey. "He'll have to take them over again."

"Can he take them online?" Maybe I could stand over him while I was working.

"He could take them in the period before school starts for the rest of the student body," he continued. "There's time to concern yourself with this later. Right now I think you have bigger problems."

"I'm worried about his schooling." I couldn't understand why the school advisor wasn't more focused on his grades.

While I was standing in the office, we were interrupted by a mom holding a Subway sandwich, needing Mr. Aloo to contact her son who forgot his lunch. The whole approach to child-rearing was beyond reason for me. I understood that children needed to be loved and respected, but they also needed governance. In our household, if you forgot your lunch or lunch money, you went hungry. No wonder Dylan struggled; he was seeing this disparity every day. I knew Dylan had forgotten his lunch today, and I was there at lunchtime with no sandwich. Why would anyone ever remember to bring their lunch if Mom was going to bring one to school? Even if I wanted to act like this, I couldn't.

On top of all the other issues in our lives, it was made more complex by the fact that I don't drive due to my severe visual impairment. I had hydrocephalus as an infant, commonly referred to as water on the brain. It crushed the optic nerve. I see well enough to work, but I do not see well enough to drive. Getting a Subway sandwich would entail me to walk a mile to the mall and another mile to the school and a mile home. It wouldn't be impossible but impractical at best. Most people don't know how limited the impairment is because my eyes look normal, except that one is green and one is brown.

My parents expected me to function normally with few considerations for my impairment. Most of the time I felt like it is as much a blessing as it is a curse. I, like many people with other abilities, learned to be creative in finding work-arounds. Most of the time I told myself that; the word *disability* implies the person has no abilities, which is, in fact, incorrect. For a second, while watching this mom and her sandwich, I hated her. I hated myself and felt sad that Dylan could not forget his lunch.

I was able to get the number for the homeschooling department before I walked back home and Dylan pretended to go to his next class. "Thank you, Mr. Aloo." His hand was warm, and he looked me in the eyes during the handshake. "Good luck to you. My door is always open."

When I got the report card with zero credits, I made arrangements to meet with Dr. Larch, the director, that led the home school program. He agreed to meet us even though he was resistant to Dylan being admitted into the program as a freshman. His practice is to let kids struggle a little longer in the regular school because sometimes students acclimate and succeed. I was still shaking from the heated argument required to get Dylan to the meeting. I was trying to calm down while sitting at the round table with Dr. Larch, Dylan, and Craig. Dr. Larch was a tall no-nonsense middle-aged man. Craig, the ever optimistic, was pleasant and the most reasonable. I wasn't doing a very good job of calming down; I was visibly angry. My shoulders were up around my ears with a furrowed brow.

The argument was loud and two against one. When I had discussed this education plan with Craig the week before, he agreed with me, but with Dylan making his case for another chance in the high school, Craig was having second thoughts. I started yelling with a familiar frustration. Craig and I had discussed this at length, and yet here he was, arguing Dylan's point of view in front of Dylan. The more we argued, the taller Dylan stood. It had taken a colossal effort to get the meeting at the continuation school as the enrollment was impacted, and I couldn't guarantee I would get another meeting. The amount of effort exerted to get us sitting at the table had left me with a dry mouth and on the verge of tears.

Dylan was being particularly abusive, hoping that if he was too abusive, Dr. Larch would deny him admission. He was cursing at Dr. Larch and telling him that he didn't need to be there. He informed everyone in the room, "My mom is crazy."

The doctor looked at the two of us and said, "That might be true, but she is fighting a war that you need her to win." He gave us the class schedule and told us to come in the following day to meet with the teacher who would give us the assignments for home schooling. He looked at Craig and wished him luck.

I Learn Geometry

Dylan and I spent every day together. He listened to his music in the office and played a computer game, *Tibia*, while I worked. At first the music was loud and annoying. He was in his head-banging music phase. "Rise Against" was his favorite. Through repetition, I learned all the words. Dylan's voice was hoarse from singing all day. He was taking medication given by his medical physician. The director of the chemical dependency unit of the local hospital was treating him. I couldn't tell if the director was crazy or a genius; sometimes, it's a fine line. He looked slovenly with a wrinkled off-white shirt that had pit stains. His overall demeanor was manic with pressured speech.

We knew within fifteen minutes of meeting him that he was a former drug and alcohol abuser that took three kinds of psychiatric drugs to manage his bipolar disorder and anxiety. Apparently, this information was in his elevator speech he uses to introduce himself. We also learned that he has been sober for twenty-four years, and his three kids are successful in their careers. He gave my fifteen-year-old two prescriptions for depression and anxiety and announced that I was a codependent and if I was not careful I would kill my son.

Dylan was gleeful as we got in the car. "Told you she's crazy!" Dylan announced to his father.

Maybe the antianxiety and antidepressant medicine would be effective. The doctor was under the impression that he was self-medicating. Maybe the entire household should line up every day and take medication. Dylan was hopeful as well. Now he wouldn't have to spend his lawn-mowing money on drugs; he could take the legal ones. His girlfriend was sad that he couldn't be in the world as often anymore. I had him on a tight leash, but he could have visitors.

This arrangement was acceptable until his girlfriend cheated on him at a party by making out with one of his friends. He didn't blame her or his friend. It was my fault because I wouldn't let him attend the party. He was crushed under the humiliation; all his friends were there. He wouldn't talk to me for two weeks which made home-schooling difficult. My stubborn mule nature forced me to press on. He couldn't, or wouldn't, see her disloyalty as a disqualifier; he kept thinking about her curves and her pretty face.

Craig's dog, Lily, was keeping us awake at night by barking. We would let her outside to go to the bathroom, but she would choose to use our carpeting instead. Looking at Dylan's brokenhearted face, I thought he needed a puppy, but I couldn't justify having two dogs. Lily was sweet in that she lay at my feet all day long while I was working, but she was wrecking my carpeting, and I deeply resented her waking us up in the middle of the night. After I found a woman who wanted a Cavalier King Charles dog, I presented my solution.

"You guys, I was thinking that we could get a puppy." We were almost finished with dinner, so if this went south, they would have already eaten. I wouldn't have wasted my time making a dinner nobody ate. The response was, of course, joyful until I announced, "This would mean we would have to give Lily away."

In unison, the kids yelled, "You are so mean!"

"I know I am mean. We all agree on that, but hear me out. Lily is waking us up every night. Your dad needs his sleep, and we don't give her the kind of attention she requires. She's got that growth near her eye that needs taking care of, and we don't have the money to take care of a purebred animal." They were staring at me like I was a monster. "I found a lady who has already made an appointment for her at the veterinarian to look at the thing on her eye. She even bought her a car seat."

They weren't budging until we looked at a picture of the puppy that we were going to pick up the following week. He was a collie-blue heeler mix, a perfect dog for a boy. The mix is known for being energetic, smart, and friendly. "So Lily is leaving tomorrow. We should say goodbye tonight." Ironically, Lily got the attention she needed the day she left our home.

Dylan's humiliation kept him in the house for two weeks, but it was made easier by the puppy we named Jack. When he didn't hate me, he talked without end. We took the dog for walks in the woods for his PE requirement, even in the rain. We referred to these woods as middle-earth.

Occasionally, we would join Scott and hunt for Chanterelle mushrooms beneath the oak trees. Scott spent fifteen years working at a boys' ranch, taking troubled youth on walks and teaching them about the wilderness. After his time at the boys' ranch, he became a probation officer. Chanterelle mushrooms are distinctive with their orange flesh and false gills. Hunting through the forest, digging through the damp soil on my knees in the drizzling rain and the smell of the rotting leaves filling the air was a science, PE, and psychology class. Scott spent hours talking to Dylan about the forest.

The two men walked side by side, talking about Scott's experience as a probation officer and writing reports for local notorious criminals in our area. Dylan's curiosity moved the conversations forward with his endless questions. It turns out that Scott had participated in the land trust committee that preserved the wooded area we were hiking in; they used the wildcat preservation act. Coming away from one of these walks, Dylan remarked, "If you were to see Scott on the street, he looks ordinary."

On one of these walks without Scott, we took a different path and were lost for miles. I was getting punchy at mile ten with no food or water. Dylan was laughing at my catastrophic solutions, like eating the dog. Of course, this only prompted me to continue the rhetoric so I could listen to him laugh; I forgot that his laugh starts in his belly.

I was with him every waking hour. I even left the office for three hours every Wednesday to walk with Dylan to school to meet with his teacher. Mr. Rogan's dedication was evident in his every action. He had no care in his appearance. He wore the same orthopedic socks with Velcro shoes and the same white polo shirt and khaki shorts every time I saw him. His long gray hair was always in a ponytail, and he listened to Dylan with every pore. He always found common ground. I had never taken geometry in school; I didn't even properly pass Algebra. So the opportunity to learn geometry with this man as he taught Dylan was fun.

It looked like Dylan was turning the corner, so we lengthened the leash to include some outings with boys we knew. I made Dylan take Jack with him because I thought the responsibility of Jack would keep him in line. One of them was his friend Travis; I didn't think he would catch him on fire twice. He was a nice boy with endless please and thank-you. Travis is the boy that Dylan had his first physical fist fight when he was in the fifth grade. I wouldn't let him spend time with Kyle though because Kyle had been in juvenile hall for drug possession. The adventures started out as trips to the movies. I wanted to encourage his good behavior with a $20 bill to pay for the movies and popcorn. He came home on time and thanked me for the trust and the money. Dylan was happy as he kissed me good night and went upstairs to bed.

Going to bed, I was bubbling over with self-praise while chastising Craig for not believing in the program. I knew that if we took control, reason would prevail. Dylan was meeting every requirement for earning his small freedom back. He eventually earned his phone back. He brought the nicest girls to the home. They would make videos of themselves in his room, dancing to the new techno music. His brilliant smile was hard to resist. They arrived every

Friday after school, and I made sure that I had plenty of snacks and sodas. There was never a whiff of alcohol or marijuana. They were just happy being together. Dylan was so thankful for our support it would be an insult to drug test him.

He started dating a Palestinian girl, Jillian. She was not allowed to date and certainly not a boy of European descent. She was Christian, like us, but her parents had a different plan for her. The obstacles keeping them from each other were insurmountable. I couldn't figure out his willingness to make his life more complex, but I liked the girl. She adored him, and he needed to be adored.

He started buying props for his Friday-night escapades such as fog machines and strobe lights. He called the parties raves. To me, it was just weird dancing and smoking cigarettes in the backyard and talking. They loved the trampoline. I would bring out snacks in order to spy. They seemed to be talking about everything and nothing. On one particular Friday night, Dylan stopped me in front of his friends and thanked me for being such a good mom and he loved me. I was so proud of my achievement it was hard to believe that we would ever have trouble again.

Wuz Up?

The phone on my desk was buzzing with a new text. I knew I shouldn't look, but I saw Travis's message. "Wuz up?" I was confused by the messages that followed. It had indicated that Dylan had picked up enough thiz to sell to everyone coming over to our house that evening. I learned from Urban Dictionary that thiz is a more powerful version of Extacy.

I regretted looking at the phone the moment I did it. It just meant I had to stop the work I was doing and address the issue. Of course, Dylan denied that the text was for him.

"I've been in bed this whole time." He didn't go for the morning hike because he wasn't feeling well and asked if he could stay home and sleep. "He probably meant to text someone else. You just don't text, Mom, so you don't understand that it's easy to text the wrong person accidently. It's a big problem. I swear, Mom, I don't want to violate your trust. It's too important to me."

Travis had to be watched; he was a drug dealer despite his clean-cut angel boy image. Craig showed me how to scroll through the other text messages which informed me that no one was who they presented themselves to be. The girl wearing the tightest dresses was a straight A student. She frequently declined party invitations because she needed to study for tests. Kyle, despite his appearance, was a heavy user, but not the supplier. Molly, the heavy girl that dressed in sweats and a T-shirt, performed sexual favors for everyone. Jillian was increasingly devoted and, according to the text, encouraging Dylan to "stay out of trouble so I can see you."

Homeschooling had the desired effect of limiting his public exposure, but the isolation was taking a toll. He complained about loneliness constantly. In some ways, the complaints were a sign of recovery. When Dylan was four years old, he was so shy and scared we took him for a psychological exam because he was hiding under the table in preschool. The psychologists thought that he had signs of Asperger's syndrome but wasn't clear if he met all the criteria. Looking through a different lens of this situation, it could be said that he was whipping Asperger's ass.

Sun Tzu, in *The Art of War* rule, teaches, "Know your enemy." Taking hospitality to a new level, I let him have his friends over, but there would be a drug test afterward. Jillian was a regular on Friday nights, which was good for him. She hung on his every word and laughed at all his jokes but spoke few words herself. She was hard to get to know, and when I asked Dylan what he liked about her, the answers were more about how she made him feel than her personal qualities. He passed the drug tests, so it seemed to be a win-win for everyone, except Robbie, his ten-year-old brother, who had to learn to pee in a cup to pass Dylan's drug test.

I was getting up earlier, 5:00 a.m., so business wouldn't suffer. Craig and Uncle Danny were planning their ascent up the World Poker Tour ladder. They were playing online poker tournaments three to four times a week. The tournaments were taking place in the middle of the night so both men could still keep their working hours. The IRS wanted a plan for us to pay the past due taxes that went underpaid the year before. The medical bills were out of control; we were adequately insured before Parkinson's diagnosis, but apparently, health insurance is for the healthy. Claire and Robbie were taking a back seat, and I had no ability to change the circumstance.

I justified Claire and Robbie taking a back seat by telling myself they were young, not in danger, and I would make it up later. I asked Robbie about it once. He looked me squarely in the face and told me, "Mom, I am going to make you drug test me all the time." He was only ten years old but understood that I was testing Dylan because I love him. I told him, "Baby, I hope not because I can't do this again."

One Saturday morning, Craig and I woke up to make coffee and walked by two young men in the hallway that we didn't know. They were much older than Dylan, who was still sleeping upstairs. They were nice enough and explained that they had met "the crew" downtown last night. When we went to bed, Dylan and his friends were playing video games in his room. They must have left the house after we went to bed. The tallest one introduced himself as Avatar. There was some confusion as we thought his mom named him Avatar before the movie even came out. He explained that the name was his street name. The other young man was quieter. They were old enough to graduate from high school but hadn't. Both were recently released from the foster care system as they had aged out. They were definitely older than eighteen, but we couldn't guess how much older. Currently they were homeless.

Craig, ever generous, made everyone breakfast. We learned a lot about "the crew," listening to them talk among themselves as we were serving them more orange juice and pancakes. I bookmarked some of their words to look up later in Urban Dictionary. If I wasn't so anxious for my son, I would find the language creative and funny; the slang is clever.

The intel-gathering breakfast was successful. It turns out that Molly is a girl in the group and also a slang word for Extacy. Thinking back on the search through his text messages, I wondered if I was confusing for the girl for the drug. The love doctor wasn't the guy who gave relationship advice; it is the drug dealer. This would be a practice we employed whenever possible. They forgot we were in the room. It bought us two things: a measure of loyalty from his friends and information.

After everyone left, Dylan failed the drug test. Robbie was spending the night at his friend's house. There was marijuana, meth, and opioids. Thiz is a concoction made by someone who has never passed even a high school chemistry class. True to form, he argued with the drug test. The pink lines that noted the negatives were obvious. The positive indicators have no lines. He insisted, "You're just blind, Mom." It is true that my visual impairment that prevented me from driving was an issue in my life, but there was no line. I know there was no line because I took his cup of pee to every other person in the house that has twenty-twenty vision. He also argued with them.

His room had two new holes in the walls and cigarette burns in the new carpeting. The burns were not just surface burns you could shave off the top; someone had put their cigarette out in the carpet. I didn't know that this kind of disrespect existed. We slowly dismantled his room. Every book, video game, dresser, bed, and piece of clothing was put in the garage. His books had carve outs where he stored drugs. Maybe he had been watching too many prison movies. I was both impressed by his creativity and scared by his determination. When we were finished cleaning his room, he had a mattress on the floor with one blanket and no doors. His bathroom provided no privacy.

After all this was done, he hugged both of us. "Thanks for doing this." He said he was relieved and committed to getting clean.

He was clean for a few weeks. We were so proud of our parenting, even allowing ourselves to go out one Friday night to have dinner with friends. We came home to Dylan's room full of drunken teenagers passed out on his floor. He could fit more people in his room with no furniture. This cycle would continue—bursts of hope interrupted by reality for years. Avatar was among the boys and was friendly when he woke up.

All his friends seemed nice enough, but I worried endlessly that these boys were sleeping in the room next to my pretty thirteen-year-old girl. Robbie's room was across from mine, but I was a heavy sleeper. I wasn't assured that Robbie was safe from these strangers. I was working twelve-hour days and managing the home as well as the business. I fell into bed every night like I had been unplugged.

The arguments were more volatile with occasional police involvement. The school was being pushed to the side, and Dylan was getting bolder and bolder in his confrontations. When I started my research into therapeutic boarding schools, it was just imaginings. I couldn't afford them; they were between $50,000–90,000 a year. I was struggling with the mortgage already. I was investigating the possibility of renegotiating my mortgage and IRS debt, but the chances were slim for either entity negotiating. I had enough money that they could see the possibility, but not enough money to meet my obligations.

There were no therapeutic boarding schools in California because the child laws in California do not allow for a child to be held against their will. It would require leaving the state and the cheapest schools are out of country. Mexico and the Bahamas were popular destinations but not optional because there were no laws in these locations that prevent the withholding of food and water. In fact, beatings are not even out of the question in these locations. At this point, I felt that Dylan deserved a beating but probably would not be therapeutic. Nevada and Utah seemed the most reasonable option. They were within driving distance and had reasonable child laws.

I interviewed several schools and landed on the one that seemed to be the most focused on the family and academics. The owners were Mormon, and therefore, faith would be a part of the program. Their website was professional. The front page of the website showed well-groomed smiling teenage boys riding horses in their equine therapy program. Some of the photos showed students hiking with the sunset behind them. They had backpacks, suggesting overnight trips. The testimonials were glowing.

"This school saved our family," one father commented. "I learned how to be a better parent." Maybe this was the answer. Dylan could get his head together, and we could regroup in a new living situation. When I talked to the school, they stated that most boys had to stay a year, but some students graduated in three months. Dylan would be on the three-month plan. That would give Dylan some skills he could use in his future, and I wouldn't have to worry about him while I focused on the short sale of our home and move our business.

They had a finance program that would allow us to pay monthly payments. I was hesitant to pull the trigger without giving Dylan one last chance. We showed him the website and gave him one month to prove he could turn his behavior around. He dismissed us "like we were small" when we were done with the conversation. The following month can only be seen as Dylan daring us to send him. He stepped up his disrespect and smoked in the house and put the cigarette out on the coffee table. He left the home without telling us where he was going and who he was with. School stopped altogether, and he called us names every day. His favorite attacks were those that made fun of our physical features. His insults were particularly creative and cruel, making comments about my being *blind* and calling his dad a crippled old man.

It isn't that I am unaware of our situation. I had joked frequently that we should call our appraisal company the Shaky and the Blind. To hear the insults come from a person that came out of my body was more disabling than my physical limitations. I worried people could see the internal bleeding when I was in public. I monitored my facial expressions when I couldn't avoid public appearances. I couldn't figure out how to the answer the simple question, "How are you?" Do I lie and say, "Fine. How are you?" or do I tell the truth? I settled on "I'm hanging in there. Let's talk about you."

People were beyond compassionate when I did talk about it, but the entire conversation was absorbed with the topic of out-of-control teenagers or drug addiction. My favorite stories were of people's recovering relatives; they were inspirational. The flip side of these stories, however, were the dead relatives. Some folks thought it was helpful to tell me the dangers of drug abuse by telling me about their losses after years of struggling with their loved ones. These were not helpful for me. Potentially, it was helpful for them to be able to tell another person who understood their pain, but I didn't need to know the dangers.

Once we figured out that Craig needed to stand in the bathroom while he was taking the drug test, he failed every one of them. So we stopped wasting our money on the tests. We begged and warned Dylan to stop. There were tears, promises, and negotiations. We threw a Hail Mary pass by telling him that we would stop caring about mari-juana and alcohol if he just went to school.

A few weeks after meeting Avatar, he committed an armed robbery at the local Walgreens and was running toward our home for safety when the police caught him.

Discovery

Robbie became anxious after Dylan was sent away; his ten-year-old self couldn't comprehend that a parent could send a child away. He asked thousands of questions about Dylan and his progress; he started his Dylan letters as soon as he finished the last one. Claire was sad, but not surprised. She had more a bird's-eye view of Dylan's behavior than I did because she was in the room next to his and knew that he was not being honest when he said he was just smoking a little weed and sometimes got drunk.

The relief was immediate for me. I knew that Dylan was safe and could move our home and business to a smaller home without having part of my brain distracted with his whereabouts. We moved across town into a condo with a pool in the project. We chose the condo because the grounds were well maintained with flowers and the pond in the middle of the project had frogs and turtles. The unit only had three bedrooms, but the rent was affordable and within walking distance of the high school Claire would be starting in the fall.

We were downsizing by half of the square footage which meant that we were going to release half of our belongings. Craig came home from the gym one morning to find me throwing the kids' toys and furniture we weren't taking with us into a trailer. "What are you doing?"

"I am purging." I kept moving. "You should try it."

"You are throwing all our stuff away." He was pulling a hobby horse out of the trailer. "This was a Christmas present."

"I know. No one played with it." Taking it from his hand, I put it back in the trailer. "It sat in the closet until the dog chewed on it and ruined it."

"Did you tell the kids you were doing this?" He pulled the toy out again. "Or are they going to come home from school after you threw away all their toys?"

"That's exactly what I am doing! I am throwing all their toys away, and I don't care about them anymore!" He was hitting a sore spot in our trope. As the story goes, he has to protect the children from the careless and thoughtless mother who does not care about their happiness. The mother who works too much and is overcontrolling.

"You are throwing away this chair?" He was pulling on the chair when I grabbed the chair.

"This chair is dangerous. We repaired it three times, and it keeps breaking. Let it go." He let it go. "Why don't you try it? It's fun." I put a broken truck in his hand. "Throw it!"

Ten minutes into this exercise, he was roaming through the house, looking for stuff to throw away. The idea of starting new was exhilarating. We took five trailers full of failed Christmas presents and things we had been holding too long. It made me rethink Christmas and my relationship with the landfill. My meditation teacher, Doris, told me to "let go with love." I don't know if I could be gracious about losing everything, but I did plant the tulip bulbs I had stored so that the next family would be surprised in the spring.

Even though we were broke and frequently eating ramen noodles with egg and peas for dinner, we were peaceful. We couldn't afford the therapeutic boarding school but couldn't afford the disruption of an out-of-control teenager. As we put our home and business back together, the silence was deafening. The chaos of the previous year had become the new normal.

Our dinner table was cleared at least three times a week to play our favorite game, Rummikub. We call Rummikub a tile rummy game, Pick and Tap, because the retirement community that Craig's mom lived in before she passed would say pick and tap. Essentially, it's a nice way of saying, "Stop wasting time." When there is nothing in the player's hand to play on the board, the player needs to pick a tile from the pile and let the next person play. The retirement community tapped because they were hard of hearing, and the act of tapping the tile is also visual. We played Pick and Tap for hours, but there were other games that we alternated with but Pick and Tap is a nice way to remember Grandma. We never played Monopoly. The kids play with their dad, but not me. Monopoly does not end well. There are tears and hurt feelings, and occasionally, the board and pieces are thrown to the floor.

We were allowed to e-mail letters to Dylan every day, but he could only e-mail us on Sundays. We waited with eagerness to read his letters which were funny and upbeat.

We were invited to participate in the three-day discovery workshop in Las Vegas. The workshop was free, but the cost of missed work and traveling stretched our limited resource. Craig had sworn off gambling, so that was not a concern, and we stayed in Craig's sister's home, which saved on the hotel expense.

The workshop started at eight in the morning and went until midnight every day for three days. The leader was an intimidating tall überconfident man who insisted that we stand at attention when he walked into the room to the music of 2001 Odyssey. His *groupie* volunteers, women wearing kitten heals and carefully applied pink lipstick, looked at him with adoration. His command of the room was objectively impressive. He belittled these rich parents with abandon.

The leader delighted in humiliating the vice president of a Fortune 500 company by telling him that the reason his son was addicted to drugs is because he was too busy being important to pay attention to his son. I watched the powerful man dissolve into a puddle of tears and then agree to sign his son up for another year in the program and then sign him and his wife up for the next three seminars at the cost of $1,500 per seminar per person. The program dug into our childhoods and the impact our childhood wounds have on our ability to raise our children. It was designed to hit all our soft spots and shine a light on the consequences of our actions or inactions.

I was not the only woman in the room wearing shabby clothing. I did the best I could, while digging through my closet, to pack, but my wardrobe is the last place I spent my money. One of the drawbacks of working from home is that I could wear sweats every day and my church doesn't care what I wear as long as I show up. There were a few other women that were having trouble affording this life choice. One woman told me she mortgaged her home while she was learning to be an ambulance driver because her son was dealing drugs from her home. She seemed to be the only one in the room capable of handling the leader. When he scolded her for chewing gum, she scolded him for being petty and vindictive. The next session, I sat next to her.

By the second night nearing the midnight hour, I was trembling with emotional exhaustion. I fell apart during the last exercise and couldn't stop crying. All the pressure of the last year and this giant of a man picking at my tender spots overwhelmed me. The other parents were compassionate and loving, but I was humiliated. I don't cry in public and I certainly don't let other people see me cry an ugly cry with snot and makeup running down my face. So when Craig stood up to commit to another workshop across the country the following month, I told him to sit down and shut up. Next month's workshop was not free and we would miss more work.

At some point in the program, we were all lined up against the wall and told to cross the room but could not use the method that another person has used. The first person walked across normally. By the time all one hundred of us crossed, the last person was cartwheeling across the room. The point of the exercise was to demonstrate if we wanted to go to the next workshop we needed to be creative in our solutions. Potentially, I should have paid attention instead of being annoyed by the manipulation.

The workshop was effective for Craig; he was not overwhelmed in the same way that I was. I was wrong. I thought we couldn't afford the follow-up workshop or the time off work, but in fact, Craig went back to gambling after the workshop and gambled the money it would have taken to do both the traveling and the cost of the workshop. Potentially, the workshop would have helped him address his gambling addiction. I would not have attended the discovery workshop if it had not been a qualifier to attend the family weekend three weeks after the workshop. I, as a rule, don't like talking about my feelings, even with my own therapist. I would rather sit naked in front of those people than to expose my private self. I have a violent history that I am hesitant to talk about. Historically, when people learn of my past, they treat me differently. I spend a lot of time trying to be normal. Whatever that is.

I spent three years going to therapy twice a week, attending to my history and the effects of the violence. I was diagnosed with PTSD and did a year of rapid eye movement therapy. Eventually, I learned to be grateful for my circumstance. Because the violence was over-the-top, I had to seek treatment at twenty-five years old. I was not able to function because I was having several anxiety attacks in a day. I spent the three years taking everything out of the box and then repacking it. The advantage is that I know myself better than most people know themselves. I know many people who had bad childhoods but can still function, so they don't seek treatment and don't have the self-knowledge that comes with good therapy.

The school had merged ten days after Dylan's arrival with the Utah campus. I felt tricked; I chose Nevada because it was closer to us than Utah. I could not bring him home after only ten days, however. We had already committed to three months of payments. We had not spoken to him on the phone, but the letters home indicated that he was doing well. Jody, his advisor, was less impressed with his progress. He was still a level 1. The most minimal effort was required to move up to a level 2 and would be expected within the first month.

Apparently, Dylan did not do his discovery workshop with the same enthusiasm his father had done his. It was, in fact, the same workshop that we had done, and Dylan hardly spoke. I didn't know what they expected from a fifteen-year-old boy. I found it challenging, and I was a woman in my forties. I would have been concerned if he had been eager to discuss his feelings, so I was not holding it against him that his progress was slow.

I Would Rather Sleep in the Dirt

I cried leaving Utah; for forty-eight hours, I had all three of my kids in the same state. We had such a good time as a family attending the parent-child workshop. I hadn't seen Dylan in two months. The long hair and baggy pants Craig dropped him off with were replaced by a military cut and a tie. His face was covered in pimples with the fatty foods they feed the kids. I failed in my effort to stay strong when I saw him. I didn't want my vulnerability to be used against me, but I cried like a baby.

He smiled when he saw Craig and me, then gave Claire a long hug. He crumpled when he saw Robbie though. According to his letters home, his biggest regret was his failure as a big brother. When Dylan was on track, he played with his brother for hours and took him to the movies. He loved sneaking Robbie into PG-13 movies. For years, Dylan walked to pick Robbie up from school and listened to Robbie prattle about his day and his friends. I was encouraged by this display.

We did some workshop, but each day, we got to spend four hours off campus. As we hiked in Zion National Park, which is a fifteen-minute-drive from the school, Dylan told me at least a hundred times that he loved me. He apologized for burning the Bible. I listened while the kids were talking among themselves. Claire showed him pictures of our new home and told him that I had planted flowers in pots on the rear deck so that our house would be beautiful like our old one. Claire and Robbie talked about walking to Target, In-N-Out, and Denny's. They talked about the dog and people at the church that were asking about him.

People noticed he was missing from church. We did not tell most people the truth because we didn't want to have to explain why we felt compelled to sell our home, drug our child, drive him across state lines, and hold him hostage. We never met anyone who had done anything like this. We told some people that he was in college preparatory school. It wasn't that far-off. He was never going to go to college on the path he was on. At this rate, his college money was going to be bail money. The few people that did know the truth were supportive.

As we walked along carefully crafted trails among the reddish sandstone structures, Dylan was feeding me all the lines I wanted to hear as if we were in a play and both of us were playing our parts. I knew it was a fantasy, but I indulged my hunger to hear the words. The school prepares parents for this exact moment with surprising accuracy. They reminded parents that kids are doing their job by being manipulative and we needed to our job by setting firm and loving boundaries. I hesitated to argue and destroy the magic. The light breeze added to the surrealistic moment. I was absorbed by colors that can only be seen in nature and listening to words I craved. I wanted my family to be whole.

The kids chattered at the dinner table like they used to do before the drugs. When they walked, they were all in a line, shoulder to shoulder, their stride in sync. My heart swelled with hope. It was hard to leave him at the school to go back to our hotel. Before I left him, I gave him a password to write in the weekly letter if he was being abused at the school. The school reviewed incoming and outgoing letters and edited the letters at will if found to be unhelpful. He was warned to only use this in an emergency. The password was "I miss peanut butter and jelly sandwiches." Because he hates peanut butter and jelly sandwiches.

The hotel was the cheapest hotel in the area because we were still eating top ramen at home. I couldn't sleep the first night. I was reliving the day. Dylan's behavior was exactly the behavior we were wanting in our home. He was clear in his communication. There were a few moments of potential arguments, but he handled them with care. I finally fell asleep when I woke up to a scratching on the bathroom tile. I still had my contact lens in my eye and could adequately see the giant roach challenging me to a duel. Of course, I woke up everyone in the room when I screamed. The kids were laughing at my hysterics. Craig was irritated but bravely battled the roach on my behalf. It was harder for me to sleep as I kept thinking about roaches in my bed or in my hair; I have a phobia of roaches. The struggle is real.

In that sleepless night, I wrestled with the decision to let Dylan come back home. He was saying all the right things and constantly smiling. He talked about Jillian and how much he missed her. He promised that he would stay clean and sober, but I had been down this road with him before dozens of times. I was worried that if this were a trick, I would have trouble getting him placed back in the program. I wouldn't be able to afford a mistake.

In the car back to the school, the kids asked if I was going to bring him back home. Craig's vote was a yes to bring him home. "He's doing so good, but what do you think?"

"I think he sounds good, but he hasn't started any of his program work. Jody says the only reason that we are here is that the next parent-child program is three months away, but Dylan should not have qualified. He has not even started his homework. He's still at level 1. It is so easy to move to level 2, and he won't do it."

"Mom, maybe the homework is too hard. Sometimes, my homework is too hard." Robbie's small voice from the back seat was hard to hear, but his message was clear; he wanted his brother home.

"I know. I want him home too, but I want him to be okay too." I was surprised Claire hadn't spoken up yet. She usually has something to say about everything.

"Let's see how today goes." I didn't think I would change my mind but didn't want to start the day with an argument.

I was also concerned with Craig's behavior during the workshop. He was more tearful than usual. I wasn't the only one who noticed. The group leader, during one of Craig's many suggestions to change the program, asked him with an edge in his voice, "What's up with you?" Craig had more sobriety than any other person in the room. He had been a circuit speaker in AA. I met Craig in his recovery bookstore. The program wasn't run like AA though. I couldn't speak to Craig during the program as husbands and wives weren't allowed to be in the same group discussions. He answered my inquiries with vague answers, so I could only let my imagination run wild. Looking back, I know it was weighing heavily on him that he started gambling again.

The boy and father sitting in front of me during one of the exercises were discussing the boy's latest infractions. He had consensual gay sex with another boy. The boy shrunk in shame next to his father, but the father put his arm around him and told him to keep his hands to himself. I realized that I was not alone in this situation. Some parents wholeheartedly supported the dogma, but some of us were just looking for a place to park an out-of-control teenager.

During one of the program activities in which we had to rate our commitment to the program on a scale of one to five, with five being the most committed, I rated myself a four. I was committed to my son, and I was willing to sacrifice a lot to keep my son safe, but I was not sure if this program was the answer. Jody called me out in front of all the other parents and told me to go stand with the twos. In the two corner was one other parent who was removing his son the next month.

I hate being the center of attention. I don't even like standing next to the person at the center of attention, which is why I did as I was told without any pushback. Craig was angry however; he argued that I had sold my home so that we could be there.

"Are there any other people in this room who sold their home to be here?" He was looking at the others with tears tracing the deep crease in the side of his face.

Jody turned toward him as did everyone else. I wondered, *Where is a trap door when you need one? How can I get out of here right now?* "It's nice you are coming to her defense."

I was praying that she wasn't going to pull our covers in front of everyone. Was she going to spill our family problems out on the floor so everyone can pick through and examine them like items in a garage sale?

"No, no, it's okay. I am okay here. This guy seems like a nice guy. I'll just stand here and talk to him." Jody responded. "Let me tell you why I put you in this category." Humor wasn't going to work here even though people were laughing. She was going to make me address this in front of everyone. "You haven't fully committed."

"Okay, you are right. I am committed to my son, but I haven't fully committed to this program. Our contract is up next month and I haven't re-upped." My voice was surprisingly clear and strong. "I don't know if this program works yet."

The woman who just committed to a third year for her sexually active daughter in group 5 standing next to Craig gasped as if I passed gas in yoga. The guy standing next to me uttered an amen under his breath. Her answer was a long and drawn-out reasoning designed to make me an example of my questioning the program. This criticism was not new to me.

Thank God the answer to my inner conflict came at breakfast the next day. Dylan was working on me telling me that he was doing well and that I had overreacted by sending him there to begin with. He told me that I didn't know what normal was because we had been sober for more than twenty years apiece. He insisted that he was only there because he smoked a little weed and drank some-times. I knew from one of his party friends that he was very involved with hard drugs and he had shared in group of the drug use. His counselor had already spoken to me regarding the drugs.

I might have even managed the drug use. His argu-ment that he has a right to do with his body what he wants is a valid point. The volatile behavior fueled by the drug use is the actual problem. I have a parental responsibility to keep him safe even from himself. Truth be told, though, I might be able to do what some of the other moms do and not look. I asked Louis's mom one time what she was doing about Louis's drug use. Louis was a classmate who spent many Saturdays nights in our home. She looked at me with astonishment because she didn't know Louis did drugs. I had never seen him sober or not high. I envied her.

The fact that Dylan wasn't able to own his behavior was the answer I was looking for. It would have been nice to come home with him and have him be a nice productive citizen, but that was a fairy tale I couldn't afford. Dylan was frustrated and made comments as we were leaving to his siblings about how I was paranoid and brainwashed by the program. I wasn't sure the program was effective for him. I knew that it was effective for the rest of the family; we were living peacefully. I thought the program was planting seeds and giving him tools for later. I doubted it was possible to halt addiction so early in the disease. He was only fifteen years old.

Before we left him at the school for at least another three months, we took him to the hotel where we groomed him with facials. Apparently, Bioré nose strips and playing cards are trading commodities in the school. I was conflicted touching his face. He hadn't let me do anything for him in years, and I was making it more difficult for myself at the end of this visit by having to leave him. He cried when we left, but I was able to stay composed until I got in the car.

I left him with twenty-five books that were required reading for California high school students. One of my concerns was that he would fall behind in his education. I couldn't give him science in the program. I knew he was taking an algebra 2 class online and a grammar class, but they didn't provide literature. He read two to three books a week in the program. Jody limited his reading because he was using his reading to avoid his issues. Before we left him at the school, we took him shopping for necessities.

Initially, Craig thought we could drive straight through but Craig was exhausted and needed to make an unexpected stop. I called several hotels passing through Nevada in hopes of finding an affordable option. I was quoted $75 by a Raddison Hotel just outside the desert. The hotel looked much nicer than a $75-per-night hotel. I was certain I wouldn't wake up to a cockroach, and if I was more alert, I might have questioned the rate. We slept for five hours and got up in the middle of the night to continue on. In fact, the rate quoted was too good to be true. The rate was actually $175 per night, which is more than we had in our checking account, and we had no credit left on the cards.

The middle-aged woman at the desk took pity on us and not only charged us the $75 but packed a breakfast and lunch for us in brown paper bags. Sometimes it pays to look pathetic. To be fair, Robbie's eyes are bluer than Dylan's, and his sleepy head is beguiling. I am frequently a captive servant to his impish face. The kids were standing at the desk barely awake and waiting to be excused so they can get in the car and sleep.

We yelped the hotel we stayed in Utah when we got home. One of the reviews was, "I would have rather slept in the dirt." We all agreed that we too would have rather slept in the dirt. We felt victorious for being strong as a family. Robbie and Claire confessed that they were worried we were going to bring Dylan home before he was ready.

I Want My Money Back

Every Wednesday, we called Jody at 11:00 a.m. and talked to her for fifteen minutes regarding Dylan's progress. Our initial three months was extended to six months after the parent-child workshop. The typical time allotted for recovery by most professionals is no less than one year. We figured if he could turn around and prove he could live in our home peacefully, we could save money and time. I knew that it didn't benefit the school to tell me he's all better after three months, so I let Dylan's letters guide me.

Jody was not impressed with his recovery. She kept commenting that he was not participating in group, but I didn't think that was as important. I wanted him to take responsibility for his behavior, but I wasn't seeing evidence of change in the letters home. He kept the same drumbeat over and over. We had overreacted to his normal teenage behavior. I tested this theory by asking other parents of teenagers if their children were destructive in their homes and if their teenager had ever called them four letter words. Typically, their eyes were wide with shock as they denied such behavior is normal.

Finding sensibility in child-rearing was made more complex by our environment. Craig and I had both grown up before the strict child laws were in place. I knew perfectly well that my parents brought me into this world and they could take me out of this world. I grew up worrying that my stepmom would kill me. I knew that my childhood wasn't normal, so I couldn't use it as a yardstick for measurement, but I didn't think my neighbors were doing it right either. We were living in a neighborhood of affluent people with college savings accounts and everyone having the latest iPhones and semiannual trips to Disneyland. Every weekend was spent on either soccer or baseball fields. The parents compared SAT scores and tutors.

I couldn't figure out how they afforded the expensive phones for the children in a recession. I was still working seven days a week, ten to fourteen hours a day. The medical bills were piling up. Craig was a candidate for a new Parkinson's treatment called deep brain stimuli. We were fortunate to live thirty miles from San Francisco where the procedure was perfected. We had to pay down the medical bills before we acquired more. We were inadequately insured and not able to change health insurance policies with preexisting conditions. Craig worked as much as his condition allowed.

I failed to notice the signs and symptoms of his gambling. I wasn't looking at the checking account. I believed him when he said he left his phone in the car. I believed him when he said he was stuck in traffic. The time and money needed to feed the addiction were readily made available until it wasn't. In two months, he gambled every dime we had in the checking account, in the safe, and in my underwear drawer.

I was standing at the check stand at Safeway with a basketful of groceries when my card was declined. I left my groceries and walked to the bank to check my balance, all the while chastising myself for my stupidity and feeling guilty. When Craig was diagnosed, after many months of ruling out other conditions and diseases, the neurologist gave him a medication that has a side effect of compulsive gambling. She spoke to me privately and made me commit that I would notify her if there were signs of out-of-control gambling. Our first significant argument when we moved in together was about gambling.

I should have told her that he already had a gambling problem, but my denial, disguised as hope, told me that it would be okay. The medication, despite the side effect, is the most effective at controlling tremors. I thought about the kids and the business, and I didn't want to do that all by myself. I was already responsible for running the house, business, and child care, but I wanted help. The lenders I did business with could be brutal when they didn't get the results they wanted with threats of nonpayment. Frequently, they claimed that we were incompetent because I was telling them something they didn't want to hear. I wanted to have a partner that was as strong as possible.

The doctor and I had this conversation four years ago on diagnosis day right after I learned that he had Parkinson's disease. I was not going to be disloyal by admitting that he had a gambling problem and couldn't have the medicine that was most effective. As I walked outside into my new reality, I grabbed the handrail to steady myself. I wondered how this was going to affect our lives. It felt like another line in time.

I heard myself prattling on about the work of the day while the world was reorienting itself. In fact, we were relieved that it was only Parkinson's. People lived a long time with Parkinson's with good medicine and with minimal pain for most of the disease progression.

Our lives are so enmeshed that this factor couldn't be encapsulated. Like a child's mobile above a crib, once one toy is disturbed, it bumps into the other toys. We had the added component of having a family business. I committed, as I floated down the stairs, that I would try to make this an asset to our family. Before I went back to work, I made arrangements for Craig and me to hike the Grand Canyon in the fall. We are going to hike every canyon and mountain we could before he is not able.

From the bank, I walked over to the card room which was three blocks from our home. I was crying when I requested to speak to the owner; the manager sat down immediately.

"Can I help you?" He escorted me to a table in a quiet corner. This was apparently an occupational hazard for him, nonplussed by my tears and frustration.

"I want my money back or I am going to sue you for taking advantage of a disabled person!" Never mind that Craig was capable of working full-time. This was my last-ditch effort.

He was trying not to laugh at my ridiculous suggestion as he explained that if they gave every wife who wanted their money back, they would go broke. I knew that the card room owner's house was the largest home seen from the top of the hill on Highway 580. His house was so large that the residents in the city objected to the size and design, complaining that it dwarfed their homes. Logically, I knew that I was participating in a futile effort. They told me that Craig could put himself on the exclusionary list, which would prevent him from winning money in California, except in the Indian casinos because, technically, they are not in California.

When Craig and I walked into the card room several hours later, at least ten people looked up to "Hi, Craig." He was Mr. Friendly everywhere he went. He put himself on the exclusionary list for five years. I was reminded how inadequate I am at managing other people's addictions. I couldn't outsmart them. It is impossible to constantly follow them around and manage my own responsibilities. Crying, begging, and negotiating are ineffective. I borrowed grocery money and plugged forward.

Craig went to Gambler's Anonymous and I went to Gam-Anon. Gam-Anon is the sister of GA. It is the same twelve steps but for the people who are affected by gamblers. There are a lot of instructions about money and how to manage the money. The instructions were to give the gambler an allowance and take the gambler off all accounts. The more I listened, the angrier I became. I didn't want to take on more responsibility. I informed Craig that he was going to have to manage himself or he was going to have to go away. He chose to manage himself.

The honeymoon period when he went to Gambler's Anonymous, or GA, was wonderful. He was remorseful and Dylan was still in Utah. We lived for five months with no arguments, and we used the time that he would be gambling to take long walks in the woods. Dylan started working the program only after we committed to the full year. We were hoping that six months would be enough, but he wasn't taking any accountability for his behavior.

What a Weird Way to Say Hello

Christmas in our house is a big deal; Craig decorates our house for days. After an annual yuletide argument regarding money, we settle down to the business of spending too much money on things the kids have always wanted and don't need. We planned the holiday in Utah. This hotel had a nice restaurant where we could share a Christmas meal.

We broke the drive up into two parts with a stop with family in Las Vegas. The closer we got to Utah, we noticed that the drivers were reacting to Craig's driving. His driving wasn't considered aggressive in California, but in Utah, people were using indecent hand gestures when they drove past us. By the time we got to the school, we had counted six people that had flipped us off. We arrived Christmas Eve in a small predominantly Mormon town with no place to eat dinner. Even the hotel kitchen was closed.

If we had been home, we would have been coming home after the Christmas pageant at church. The church is filled to the rafters with parents trying to control their exuberant children and get them into costumes. To call them costumes is an exaggeration, more like bathrobes for the shepherds and halos for the angels. Mary and Joseph are typically the oldest girl and boy from the youth group.

Bruce opens the service with his arms opened wide, a big smile, and a warning that the service has a general direction but to expect some chaos. I usually have a stuffed chicken in the oven for dinner afterward. It's a meal that everyone likes, and I don't have to fuss over when I am trying to wrap last-minute gifts.

We found a few cheese and crackers in a gas station and ate our feast in the hotel room. We were staying in the hotel outside Zion National Park. This time, we brought Jack and put him at the doggie dude ranch because seeing Jack was one of Dylan's Christmas presents. The owner of the ranch had no intention of letting us interrupt her Christmas by letting Dylan come to his see his dog. She relented after I explained the circumstance and agreed to let us come for twenty minutes after breakfast. Our whole Christmas was planned around the twenty minutes between 10:00 and 10:20 a.m. We would be able to pick Jack up the following day and spend the whole day with him.

The long drive with Robbie, Claire, and Jack was an exercise in patience. Robbie and Claire had two physical fights which did not end well for Robbie. He is three years younger than Claire and not as willing to hit a girl. I hoped that I wasn't wasting everyone's time and effort. Dylan's letters talked about missing his dog, but I couldn't tell if this was real or manipulation. I worried that I made the kids sit in a car for thirteen hours each way with a dog that kept stepping on them, trying to get to the window for nothing. I should have trimmed Jack's toenails before we left. To make matters more interesting, Jack had counter surfed lunch meat before we left and had the meat farts.

My concerns were unfounded. When we got to the doggie dude ranch, the reunion between boy and dog was joyful. Jack's fat body wiggled all over when he saw Dylan, and tears were streaming down my son's face. The ranch owner was crying right alongside Craig and me, telling us that this was a gift to her, and invited us to take the dog with us and she would welcome us back before dinner. We couldn't walk the dog into Zion National Park, so we walked Jack on the outskirts of the park and drove inside the park.

Dylan's stories of the school were hilarious and disturbing. One of the group activities is to invite people into a circle when they recognize their own behavior. Mostly it is for activities like "who has stolen from your parents?" Not everyone in the program is rich; however, some kids are state funded as an alternative to juvenile detention. One of the state-funded boys walked to the center of the circle and asked the question, "Who has ever done a drive-by and doesn't know if you killed someone?" The boys were all standing shocked, staring at the boy standing in the center all by himself. This was next-level stuff.

The girl's portion of the school was separated from the boys by buildings and time schedules. I met some of the girls' parents in the parent groups. It seemed that normal, but undesired sexual behavior is the main reason the girls were confined in this school. A lot of the families were fundamental Christians that believe sex is confined to marriage only. I had trouble imagining sending my child away when birth control was an option. One girl's mother, during the parent portion of the last workshop, explained that

J. MARIE

her daughter had come home after a year in the program against her counselor's advice. She let her sixteen-year-old daughter skip church one Sunday and came home to her daughter in bed with her boyfriend. The girl was back in the program the next day.

I thought cutting was an after-school special topic, but not prevalent. According to Dylan, the reason that every meal had to be eaten with a spoon was to prevent the *cutters* in the room from using the cutlery from being used destructively. Apparently, it's hard to eat salad with a spoon. I didn't know Dylan ate salad. If nothing else came from this school, Dylan learned to eat vegetables. These stories made it hard to justify keeping Dylan in the school.

It is true that he didn't participate in drive-by shootings and is not a cutter, but his behavior was destructive. He argued that he was "not that bad." There was a tense ten minutes of his trying to argue that he didn't need to be there and me reminding him that we had tried everything we could to curb his behavior and maintain some semblance of peace in our home. No one needed to be perfect in our home, but we needed to feel safe in our home and we didn't feel safe before he left.

Despite the tense ten minutes, we all agreed that it was the best Christmas our family ever had. We ate a wonderful meal of prime rib after a whole day with the dog and time in Zion National Park. Dylan wanted to teach us a new game he had learned. Craig and I were grinning like Cheshire cats while he was teaching us spades. We pretended to learn the game. Craig and I were a team against Dylan and Claire and taught them the real game. I had

LOVING DYLAN

spent time in my using days in the ghetto of Richmond, California, playing spades all night long while drinking vodka and smoking weed. The kids did not mind that the presents were scarce that year. They all got things they needed and a few luxuries.

We had all determined that flipping people off is how people in Utah say hello. By the time we left, we counted fourteen people saying hello. Leaving Dylan again was hard. He was getting close to his return-home date. I wanted to stay longer because it was nice to be with him when he is sober. He has a curious mind and looks at life with a comedic lens. All his stories are laced with sarcasm. Unfortunately, the school views sarcasm as an act of hostility. Dylan, however, wasn't entirely sober in the school. He would drink hand sanitizer when he had access.

The Lone Ranger Rides

I woke up on a Tuesday in February with a frantic need to talk to Dylan for no particular reason. I couldn't explain my compulsion because the letters from Dylan were focused on his return home. He was nervous about coming home and the pressures that were involved. He sounded healthy and ready for life in sobriety. His nervousness was comforting because that meant he was paying attention. For the first time, it appeared that we were all on the same page. He seemed to be in line with our expectations, which were minimal. All we wanted was a teenager that wasn't wrecking our home and our family. It seemed simple.

The school was putting pressure on me to sign him up for another year. I figured if they didn't affect change in Dylan in a year, they probably wouldn't affect change in another year. They would, however, impact my bank account. I was willing to spend the money if Dylan was buying in, but he wanted to come home. He had a moment of indecision because the friendships he developed in the school were the deepest friendships he had ever had. The group therapy sessions made the boys address all their fears and insecurities at a group level.

Jody initially denied my request to speak to Dylan; it wasn't my day to talk to him. Being rude is not my primary strategy to influence, but I was forceful in my request after she denied me. I was threatening and I couldn't explain my behavior to even myself, but I was talking to Dylan within the hour.

"Mom, is Dad okay?" He was concerned because it was so unusual to be pulled out of class; he thought something had happened to one of us. His confusion made me feel foolish.

"Sorry, I didn't mean to scare you." I had no answer when he asked me why I was calling. The timbre in his voice worried me. His words were neutral. "I just wanted to talk to you. How are you?"

He was next to Jody, so he couldn't speak freely. "I am fine."

"Do you miss peanut butter sandwiches?" I continued on for the sake of covering the code talk. "I was thinking about bringing some the next time we see you." He answered negatively without hesitation. The conversation was five minutes long.

There was nothing alarming other than the sound of his voice. We exchanged I love yous, and he went back to his online lecture. Jody was giving me a lecture about overreacting. The director interrupted Jody's lecture on codependency. His voice is smooth with the consistency of brandy if brandy had a voice. The sweetness in his presentation delayed the burn of his message. He, with his finest manners, told me that my son is the worst he has ever seen.

I still don't know where I got the nerve to talk to him with no shame or fear. Typically, I would be awash in shame and sink into obedience in response to a rejection from a person with authority. He has authority in his subject, but I rejected his statement.

"I seriously doubt that my son is the worst you have ever worked with." I knew from Dylan that there were kids who had accidently killed people. I knew there were kids who were avoiding juvenile detentions in a perverted "get out of jail free" card. Because they were rich and white.

"We will be arriving Thursday morning to take our son out for the day off campus." He uttered a half-hearted argument that I disregarded and gave the instructions to have Dylan ready before 10:00 a.m.

For the first time in the business history, I returned work incomplete as we closed the business down and pulled Robbie and Claire out of school. I went to target to buy underwear for everyone because I didn't even have enough time to do the laundry. I felt silly standing in the entry of the school and Dylan looking fine. His voice still had an unknown quality, but he was smiling.

We used the time off campus to give him the option of staying if he felt like he would benefit from the extra time. I didn't talk about money. He was thoughtful in his decision-making because it occurred to him that, as boring as it was in the school, it would be scary in the real world. He made promises to us that sounded sincere if he chose to come home. I expected half of the promises to be kept, which would be a vast improvement over the behavior that was in our home before he left. The trip was only forty-eight hours long. I had angered many clients with my sudden departure.

Our regularly scheduled phone call would be potentially the last one before we picked him up for home unless he chose to stay. Both Jody and Mr. Jade, the director, were in the room to monitor the conversation.

"Hi, Mom. Jody and Mr. Jade also say hi." They did not have us on speaker phone so they could only hear his side.

"Did you think more about staying?" I was surprised he was even considering staying, but if I thought more than once about it, it was obvious. "I know you were disappointed that the school website's promise to work with horses turned out to be you shoveling poo and you don't get to actually ride them. You also spend a lot of time washing dishes, but I think the friendships have been very satisfying."

"Yeah, I learned a lot in here." This had to make the listeners happy. "It would be fun to be a level 6 in here because they get a lot of privileges and get to help run the program through peer review."

"So what would stop you from staying?" I was putting him in a tough spot with this question.

"It seems that I am punished for every little thing I do wrong, even things that other people are not punished for." I knew what he was talking about because Mr. Jade was frequently aggressive with him, trying to push him to look at his issues. Dylan's issue with the director is that he was being encouraged to express himself in the way that the director approved.

As we ended the conversation, I encouraged him to talk to the director with his real feelings, not the feelings that were expected,. but if he expressed his real concerns and feelings to the director, I would support him.

Five hours later, the director called me to inform me that I needed to take Dylan home. I explained to him that it would take a few days to get there. He stated that was not soon enough and an airline flight had already been booked and billed to me. Dylan was not to be told that he would be leaving on a 6:00 a.m. flight and any indication made to this fact in an e-mail would be subverted in the letter-review process.

This wasn't how I imagined the last day in the program. We were going to stay in the nice hotel and do some zip-lining outside of Zion before we took the long trip home. We planned to stop in Las Vegas and see family. We would all hug Jody and give her a gift card for her favorite local restaurant and coffee house. Dylan would get to say goodbye to his friends and tie everything up in a nice neat bow.

Instead, we scrambled to change our work schedule to pick him up at the airport the following morning. When Dylan saw me at the Oakland airport, he hugged me and twirled me around saying; "I was like the Lone Ranger!"

He couldn't wait to tell me the story. His conversation with the director was honest. He told the director that the program had a lot of potential, but the fact that peer approval was involved in the program led to a *Lord of the Flies* atmosphere. The director asked, "What is *Lord of the Flies*?" Dylan broke down the experience for him.

The ability to move up in the program depends on peer review. Confidence and aggression is treated equally which left nonaggressive kids standing in the cold. It created a hostile environment among the boys. Similar to the outside world, those boys that got the Rolex watches when they reached level 4 were treated with a higher regard. When Dylan reached level 4, I gave him a dinosaur watch as an inside joke. I had no idea that a Rolex was an option for anyone.

First and foremost, I didn't think the school would allow for a Rolex to be given for such a trivial milestone. Reaching level 4 just meant that you were starting to function in a productive manner. It didn't mean that you were actually productive. A $10,000 watch for a fifteen-year-old kid was outside of my reality. Dylan sat for fifteen minutes and told his truth with clarity and confidence. To the director's credit, he listened to him with minimal pushback. If the director had offered to change things, Dylan was prepared to stay for another three to six months.

The problem came during group time when Dylan stood up and started a revolt with his peers. The group leaders had been begging him to share, and when he was finally sharing his feelings, they were telling him to stop talking. He was isolated to his room and was very nervous about the next day. He was worried that they were going to *ghost* him. Ghosting is the worst punishment given in the program. The "ghost" is institutionally ignored by everyone for an allotted time. Anyone who breaks the code by speaking to the ghost is punished by being ghosted themselves.

He was delighted when they handed him a garbage bag at 4:00 a.m. to put his essentials in for the airline flight home. Jody wished him well as he got on the plane. I was nervous about his return home. I knew that sending him to the school was the best solution but was far away from perfect. Dylan was excited now but would realize that we had kept him hostage for a year. His teenage brain could not understand the position we were in, and I would pay for sending him away for a long time.

This was made evident on the way home from the airport when we stopped to meet an appraisal appointment. "Seriously, you couldn't even take today off? You are going to make me wait to get home? You are obsessed with work." His irritation was diffused as he called friends and family while waiting in the car. We didn't tell Claire and Robbie that he was coming home, so when they walked home from school together, they walked in to Dylan sitting on the couch.

Claire walked up and hugged him. "How long are you here for? I didn't know you were coming." She hugged him again.

"I am home. I am here forever." They spent the evening talking about his last few days at the school and walking around his new neighborhood.

Dylan later learned that the program changed the model of peer pressure, which created the hostile environment. He was proud of his courage. We were watching comedians on TV one day months later, and he asked me, "Why did you call me that day I was pulled out of school?" I told him I didn't know why, but I was really worried about him. I apologized for my silliness. He looked at me square in the face and told me that he had been lying on the shower floor that morning, trying to figure out if he wanted to kill himself.

Fighting the Wind

"Mom, I ran out of food stamps." It had been two days since I spoke to him last.

"You just got them. Did you sell them?" The relief in my voice was audible even through my irritation. "I can't talk right now. I am going into church, but I'll talk to you on the way home."

"Don't forget to call. I'm hungry." After a promise to return the call, I told him, "I love you."

For the first time, I understood the reality that I might not get to keep my son. Tears would show up spontaneously in my day with no advanced warning, even in public. There's not enough makeup in the world to cover the grief; my tear ducts were irritated. I would walk for miles and go to the gym every day. I kept plugged into my friends and church even when I felt like staying in bed.

My first AA sponsor twenty-something years ago kept telling me AIS, short for Ass in Seat; no matter if your ass falls off, you still come and sit in the meetings and do what you are told. I lost track of her years ago, but she still lives in my head. Our first official meeting, she handed me a leather medicine pouch with small crystals that had various purposes—rose quartz for love, hematite for grounding, and amethyst for sobriety. The bag was awkward and banged around when I ran, but I wore it for the first year of my sobriety. I have no idea if these minerals are effective, but every day I followed her directions I stayed sober. I was back to meetings and following directions like a child; eventually, my default setting was contentment instead of fear.

When my mind finally settled, a new reality appeared. It was a possibility that Dylan could die not understanding that he is loved. This fear was fueled by a statement he made in a conversation as an offhand remark. "I should have just killed myself, right, Mom? That would solve your problem." The comment was both a manipulation tactic and a request for reassurance. I stopped lecturing entirely. Telling him to stop using drugs at this point was a fool's errand, but I told him every day that I love him even while he was cursing me for not sending money.

While I was at a party, Tim, a friend I hiked Mount Shasta with ten years prior, asked if I would do it again. This was a generous offer as my vision is a factor. I have almost no depth perception. Robbie and Claire agreed to be my "seeing eye" people and help me get down the mountain. Going up is not as hard as coming down for me. I was strong enough and the heart was willing. Tim forgot the offer when I approached him with dates, and I went on with the rest of my life.

A few weeks later, at a different party, he offered to hike Shasta again, and this time, the offer stuck. I reminded him how difficult the climb had been for me the last time. I didn't even know why I wanted to do this again. One might even consider the expense of the equipment and the time off work irresponsible. The risk of bodily harm was real. Every year, at least two people who have twenty-twenty vision die hiking the mountain. I was excited for Claire and Robbie to have an adventure with me before they started their new school years.

"Okay, I am out of church and walking home. You have my full attention." It's a three-mile walk from church, and I had errands to do on the way home.

"What are you doing today?" His voice was clear as a bell.

"I can't send the money until I get home on my computer." The sky was still cloudy, but it had stopped raining. "You sound good."

"Yeah. I stopped doing the drugs." I didn't know if this was true, but I let myself believe it for now. "I just drink a few beers at night."

"Did I tell you that Claire, Robbie, and I are hiking Mount Shasta in ten days?" I was getting excited the more I did the practice hikes. "And Claire chose Santa Cruz! I think part of the attraction is that it's nearby enough to visit when she wants but far enough to be living on her own. Also, their research on astrophysics is world-renowned with NASA just a hop, skip, and a jump away from the school. She wants to work there after school."

I felt cruel saying these things when his life is in the dumps, but I wanted him to know what he was missing. "Good, I am proud of Claire." This wasn't the response I expected. Maybe he saw through my manipulation efforts, or maybe he was really proud of her with no ulterior motive.

Just to tighten the screws I answered, "I wish you were hiking with us, and if you get clean and sober, you could go on to a four-year school. You are really smart. I actually thought that you were going to be the scientist, not Claire. I remember watching a documentary about the space shuttle with you when you were three years old. You were so into it that I asked if you wanted to be an astronaut one day and fly the shuttle. You looked at me in the face and said, 'I don't want to fly the rockets. I want to build the rockets.'"

"Yeah. I thought Claire was going to be a model." His voice was thick. "Remember when she went to those modeling classes in the city and we would wander around for hours until it was time to pick her up and get back on BART?"

"Those were good days when you first came home from the boarding school before the drugs." This game of twisting each other's knives was a brutal game of intimacy. "We had so much time wandering in and out of stores with clothing we could never afford."

He was laughing. "Remember the $400,000 Rolex watch we got to try on? That guy was so nice taking it out of the safe. He knew by looking at our clothes that it cost more than our house. He must have been bored."

"Probably. He probably sells one of those a year. I wonder how many times he has tried it on. I mean, we didn't even know it existed until he told us about it when we were trying on the other watches. Actually, that watch was ugly, and I couldn't tell the difference between the cheap $10,000 watches and the $400,000 watch." We were both giggling at this good moment in our lives.

I would give my right arm just to be standing in that moment again. It had been raining that day, and he was sixteen years old and mouthy. We had a four-hour wait for Claire and $30, which would cover lunch and a coffee or a movie and shared popcorn. We couldn't decide on the movie, and a movie is only two hours, which leaves us broke and hungry, so we wandered the streets. Our clothing were getting wet, so we dipped into the mall instead of wandering around outside. We were looking for something warm to drink when we distracted ourselves in the Rolex store.

We talked the entire walk home and I transferred enough money to eat for a few days. If he chose to use the money for drugs, I couldn't do anything about it. It was beyond my abilities to hear my child tell me he's hungry and not feed him.

Claire had applied to four schools as a transfer student; UCLA, Davis, Santa Barbara and Santa Cruz. She was accepted, with scholarships, to all. She chose Santa Cruz because she was interested in the research work and the campus is beautiful. I almost bumped into a deer when I was walking around the campus. To get to her physics building, she has to pass through a redwood grove to cross a bridge dripping with wisteria flowers over a small creek with frogs. Robbie was starting his senior year and I was learning to live single after Craig and I separated. We spent months training and gathering gear. Tim and I drove up early to reserve a campsite at the base of the mountain and get our summit passes.

I had not heard from Dylan for three days and didn't want to go up the mountain until I knew he was alive. I imagined him alone in his room growing cold with a needle sticking out of his arm. Even though I paid his rent, my contact with his landlord was limited. I worried that if I asked the landlord to check on him, he might see something that could get him kicked out, but the pit in my stomach would not subside. When I finally called and asked, the response I got was chilling.

"Usually, I don't interfere, but someone should come and get this kid. He's not doing well." I was in Dunsmuir, twelve miles from Mount Shasta, eating lunch. I had spent the rest of the money on the gear in the back of the truck. Turning back wasn't an option. I could not put Dylan's crisis ahead of Claire and Robbie one more time.

"Thank you." I was aware that people could see the tears coming down my face. "Does he need to go to the hospital? His medical card is in his wallet. He has Blue Shield."

"No, he's awake. I'll have him call his dad with my phone. His phone is not charged." Dylan must look terrible. His landlord was not a warm and fuzzy kind of guy. During my visit to Astoria in the fall, the "courtyard fellas" all had words about the landlord.

Craig made arrangements to fly up to Portland and meet Dylan at the airport the next day, and they could drive down together in Dylan's car. I turned off my phone and hiked the mountain; the assent was difficult. My backpack weighed approximately thirty pounds, and snow looks like a smooth white blanket with no variance in the topography. I couldn't see the depressions in the snow and fell several times. Even though I kept my expensive sunglasses on the entire time, I still had floaters in my vision from sun exposure. Getting to base camp ten thousand feet up the mountain was like conquering the world.

When we got there, Robbie had to lie down with an altitude headache. The vista in front of us helped to shrink my problems; I was reminded that I only see a part of the picture. Part of the attraction of this trip was to exhaust myself and move my ego out of the way in order to get to the truth of the matter. From base camp, you can see as far as Lassen. I had to make a decision regarding Dylan. He was going to be homeless if I didn't give him money I didn't have for a down payment for a new place to live or let him stay in my home. He could not stay with Craig longer than twenty-one days, according to his housing by-laws. Craig was surprisingly content living alone with his dog in the Senior Living development.

After a freeze-dried dinner of chicken masala and Thai curry rice eaten from their packages, a violent wind started blowing. Our tents were only held down by the rocks we collected before the wind started in earnest. Every once in a while, a neighbor's tent would blow down the mountain with a frantic hiker chasing it. We went to bed before sunset in order to get up at 2:00 a.m. to summit.

I was scared to summit. It had been hard enough getting to base camp, and the summit was even more treacherous with long stretches of ice and snow. The goal is to summit before the sun melts the snow holding boulders in place to avoid falling rocks. We had helmets, but a falling rock is deadly. Tim let us all know if one goes we all go and if one stays we all stay. As I went into my tent that I shared with Claire, I promised to go as far as I could. It would be disappointing if I held Robbie and Claire back. The last thing Tim asked me while I was taking my boots off derailed me. He asked, "What message are you giving Dylan by calling him every day?"

There was no escaping the wind; the noise of the tent blowing was deafening. Claire fell asleep immediately, but I couldn't even close my eyes. My mind wouldn't stop. I was trapped in a dark tent with no distraction. Of course, I couldn't find my reading glasses. There was no cell phone reception. No one could hear me talking, even Claire whose warm body was right next to me. My whole body cried. The tears were irritating my already irritated eyes.

Tim's question bothered me because I respect him, and his children are confident, educated, and adventurous. I thought the message I was sending by calling every day was that I loved him even when he is not doing well. What if, however, the message I was giving him is that he is not capable? I wondered how many other ways that I was giving him this message. I went through all the efforts and sacrifice that have been made to support Dylan hoping to direct him toward a productive life. I had put him above all the other family members. His chaotic life frequently bumped into our lives with no warning. Too often, we put aside our plans and resources to right his circumstance. Keeping him alive consumed my life.

I told myself that I did this because I love him, but I had to admit I was using his problems to distract me from my own issues. I definitely love him, but I had to ask myself what letting go of him would do to my identity. Could I still think of myself as a good mother? I didn't want to throw away my son, but listening to the wind beating the tent for hours, I realized that trying to control my son was as futile as controlling the wind. Fighting the wind only exhausts unnecessarily. Wanting something is not enough. By the time Tim's alarm clock rang, I was glad to escape the tent to summit. I would rather climb a glacier than learn my truths.

As soon as we started moving around in the moonlight, Claire started vomiting all her freeze-dried food into the snow. The yellow curry in the snow almost glowed in the dark. I tried to persuade Tim to take Robbie up the summit and I would stay at base camp with Claire. His reasoning was quick and experienced. We had to head down the mountain first thing in the morning. The best treatment for altitude sickness is to decrease altitude. I was relieved to not have to summit, but I was apprehensive to go back to wrestle with God like Jacob in the Old Testament. I was lying my head down on a rock like Jacob did, except that my rock was in the shape of Mount Shasta. Maybe sleep would find me.

The wind continued to viciously rip at our tent with the nylon acting as drum fabric, and we were sleeping in the percussion piece of the instrument; it made sleep impossible. Any hope of finding my reading glasses was squashed by Claire, who was rightly grumpy with my poking and prodding. She was miserable. I lay in my own discomfort to finish my revelations. I started to wonder if I was right

J. MARIE

about Dylan. It occurred to me that my judgment regarding his drug abuse, while well-meaning, could be wrong. He had his own life with his own consequences. If I looked at the arch of my life, I can see how all my experiences have factored into the person I was today, even the bad experiences. Maybe I was standing in his way of living his best life. Maybe my mom duties had ended and the only role I had in his life was to stand on the sidelines, cheering him on, like a broken-down cheerleader.

I started wondering how I was going to let Dylan be homeless. I knew intellectually that it would be irresponsible to give him rent money that I needed for my own rent. I tried to imagine the effect that moving him back home would have on me and the other kids. I felt guilty because I didn't want him to come back home. My house was peaceful with no yelling or conflict. I couldn't figure out how letting him back home would solve his problem anyway. It seemed that it would make more problems. I consciously reminded myself that he had overdosed in my home; bringing him home was no guarantee that he would stay alive.

I wasn't ready to give up my happiness, but I kept smacking into the notion that "a mom can only be as happy as her least happy child." It's hard to be happy when my child is suffering, but at a certain level, he was choosing to not treat his substance abuse. I didn't want to wait for him to get his life in order before I could go on with my life. I knew intellectually that I had a right to be happy, but the rest of me argued with my brain.

I looked at Claire lying next to me. She was a good girl, willing to climb a mountain with me and sleep in the snow. Robbie and Claire deserved to be peaceful. Then it occurred to me to give myself the same advice that I would give Claire. I would never tell Claire to invite chaos into her life; I could treat myself like I treat Claire. The sun rises and sets on this tiny girl. She's twenty and planning her twenty-first birthday party, but she will always be my tiny girl that I would have tea parties with in the afternoons. She was going to move to finish her bachelor's degree in four months, and I didn't want to pollute that time.

I couldn't think of one time in my life that I considered myself in the equation. In my rambling mind, I thought of my priest, Bruce. His sermons were always the same message said from many different angles. "We are all children of God." The message floated past my thoughts like a life preserver. I grabbed the thought and let the message sink into my bones. My unhappiness wouldn't solve anyone's problem, even Dylan's. In fact, it seemed counterproductive. My business even does better when I am peaceful.

Sunrise was extraordinary with the full moon still visible and the snow reflecting the early-morning light. We packed up quickly. Of course, I found my readers while packing. They had been on my first layer of clothing; I could have been reading the whole time. I had not slept even ten minutes which was not helpful with my vision. I carried some of Claire's belongings down until we descended far enough down to quell her nausea. Tim followed me while guiding my every step. My vision was compromised by exhaustion and the snow glare. Taking a helicopter down would have been the only other option, and they charge you to pick you up.

Tim distracted me with chatter about his kids and his family. His daughter had just moved to Australia all by herself and was working in the world-famous Opera House. He had just come back from visiting her in her new apartment and was given the grand tour of Sydney and then they went to New Zealand to meet up with our mutual friend Scott during his walkabout. Scott had been on our first trip up Shasta. When I fell, I just popped right back up without a thought. A couple of times, Tim grabbed my backpack and set me right. After a dozen falls, I was cold, tired, and frustrated. Claire took a picture of me floundering like a turtle; I fell backward on my backpack and couldn't get back on my feet. Not my best moment.

Even though my pack was heavier, I felt like I was floating. I don't know why I couldn't figure out the simple truth without having to be held hostage by the wind. I don't control anyone's actions even if I am right. Not only do I have no control, I am also actually hurting Dylan. With my effort to control the situation, I am signaling him that I can control him and he doesn't have to figure it out for himself. I felt grateful to have the burden lifted.

I went to the eye doctor three months after Mount Shasta. I had been avoiding the doctor because my eyes had not recovered since my trip. They were strained, and of course, my thinking went straight to "You are going blind," and I would have to start making arrangements to get a Seeing Eye dog. I was worried that I might not know how to properly discipline a dog because I hadn't done a very good job with my kids. I thought that I might like to have a pretty German shepherd named Lucy. Girl dogs are probably nicer than boy dogs.

I told the doctor I was nervous. She noticed that there was damage from light exposure, but my eyes were strained because my lens was overcorrecting. My vision had dramatically improved. I still had no peripheral vision, and the other eye didn't work at all. It was still like looking through Swiss cheese because the optic nerve damage had not improved, but the part of my eye that does see was getting better with age. I know it sounds crazy, but I think it has to do with seeing my life more clearly. I had just gotten used to the idea of having a dog named Lucy.

I am not clear if I had climbed the mountain sooner if I would have had the same clarity. The story I tell myself is that I could have saved myself and my family a lot of heartache if I had learned the lessons sooner, but I think this is another fairy tale. The key ingredient is desperation; I couldn't see until I could.

Payback, Sucker!

Reentry after Horizon, the therapeutic boarding school, was difficult for the family and harder for Dylan. Robbie and Claire made full effort to set resentments aside and embrace him. Craig made arrangements to give Dylan flying lessons at the local airport. He thought if he could get Dylan high, he wouldn't need to get high. We cut back on work for the month that he came home and went whale watching in Monterey. Claire introduced him to a girl in her class. He was receptive to these efforts, but the trouble with the schooling was an obstacle.

The high school couldn't figure out how to assimilate him so late in the year, and the credits he gained while away didn't coincide with their system. His prior experience in the mainstream high school didn't inspire full cooperation either. They were less than eager to extend an olive branch. He could start a hybrid of his third year in high school in the fall. Online school was a failure, so he tested out of high school with a GED test and a promise to start classes in the fall at the local community college.

He stayed sober for a month. We found out he was not clean and sober while at a family church retreat when his weed pipe fell out of his shorts pocket. If I were to say that I handled this like an adult, I would be telling a lie. I knew that I should manage my expectations and I knew the success rate of these programs were miniscule. I tried to keep success in perspective; it could be measured by the fact that we had the year without having a disruptive teenager in the home. We had an opportunity to put our lives back in order, and we planted seeds of recovery for later. No matter how much he resisted the message, he could not help hearing it. He might not pick up the tools immediately, but he, at least, had the tools.

I could have kept my composure, but that would not have taken into consideration the overwhelming disappointment and fear. We had a very loud argument in the beautiful retreat center.

He was rummaging through everyone's suitcase; Craig was holding the pipe and little baggy in his hand. "Are you looking for this?"

"You have no right to go through my stuff!" He yelled so loud Robbie jumped.

"We have every right to go through you stuff!" My voice was just as loud. We, in fact did not go through his stuff; it fell out of his pocket when he changed on the beach.

"Why do you have it here? The agreement was that you would stay clean and sober." For a second in time, I forgot that I would have to face this genteel society downstairs and they could hear my family unravel.

"Mom, it's marijuana. It's good for you. You should try it." Was he missing the point on purpose?

"You promised. Did you mean the words when you were saying them?" I was unabashedly crying in the corner of the room.

"I would tell you anything to get out that place. It wasn't a fair negotiation." That is an obvious point I missed.

I don't remember the words that followed, but there was an exchange that was so volatile and hurtful from both sides it seemed that recovery was impossible even though it was less than one minute. Commercials are ninety seconds, and they go by unnoticed. I don't know if anyone has ever raised their voice in this setting. We were airing all our dirty laundry among people I adore and didn't want to know me in my crazy truth. I could smell the lavender through the open window as we were yelling at each other. I can hear muffled voices talking about spiritual matters as he was screaming profanities at me. There was no way I could put my face on after this, so we snuck out of the retreat early in humiliation.

After the retreat, there was open rebellion. He drank alcohol and smoked weed in the garage. We were right back where we started, except that now he shared a room with his eleven-year-old brother and we were broke. The six-panel drug tests that we gave every Saturday morning tested positive for THC only. We considered this to be a small victory. We could live with a pothead if he kept it away from his brother.

As Craig's Parkinson's disease marched on, we prepared for the cutting-edge deep brain stimuli (DBS) surgery. The surgery is designed to control the symptoms but is not a cure. We were still inadequately insured. The medical bills were astronomical, which also included the payments still being made for the school. Instead of paying another employee to drive Craig around during his recovery, we hired Dylan. He was paid well and got to spend hours with his dad at work, learning a trade. The surgery was more successful than anyone of us expected. Craig was functioning as well as he was five years earlier.

We were overjoyed when Dylan signed up for criminal justice classes at the community college within walking distance. He was spending time with another boy named Kyle. Kyle's dad was in final stages of multiple sclerosis and bedridden. The two boys bonded over broken parents. Kyle was charming but not charming enough to justify the number of friends he always had around him. He wasn't wearing a polo shirt like the last drug dealer, but he always used his manners and was quick with a smile. I asked him what kind of drugs that he sells and he told me, "Just weed." His phone rang too often for just weed, especially when medical marijuana was already legal.

We told anyone who asked about Dylan's progress that he was planning to be a police officer. We ignored the fact that he was always drunk or high, thinking that he would get his act together when school started. The first day of school was an event in our home. He left with his new backpack and computer. He was the youngest student in the classes at sixteen years old; some of the students already worked in the industry.

He seemed engaged in the subject matter, so it was surprising when he stopped going to class. He complained about being the youngest person in the class and that he would come back to college next year when he was older. He didn't quit in time to get my money back. Still, ever hopeful, I paid for another expensive online class that he didn't finish. We kept hoping and he kept weaponizing our hope. It was easy. If he started in a direction that we approved he could get full cooperation from us. This included the tools, such as computers and a used car. The pattern would continue with an excuse to not finish and then start another project.

He started working for a man who goes to our church who installs gentlemen vineyards in rich people's homes. Keith was as far right in his political leanings as I was far left. Dylan would leave my home after watching the *Daily Show*, a comedy news show that lampoons the ridiculous in the news. He would arrive at Keith's house to have coffee and watch Fox News, the source of the *Daily Show*'s comedy. He was getting out of our wacky liberal bubble.

The two men, Dylan and Keith, spent their days working in the dirt, talking about politics, and gardening. This was a good fit. Dylan was a hard worker. It was in his DNA; he comes from a long line of hardworking blue-collar people. We wouldn't buy Dylan beer or wine, but he learned to brew beer in the garage and turn any juice into wine with the right temperature and yeast.

On his days off, he would start the day with a drink of his own making. His friends complained that it was awful tasting but effective, so I was surprised when he vomited all over the stairs at eight in the morning. I was ready to take him to the hospital, thinking he had food poisoning when he admitted that he started drinking wine before it was ready and the yeast was protesting.

I happened to see my face in the mirror as I walked by with another bunch of vomit-covered towels. I was rushing to clean the mess up and manage the smell before my employee came to work. I looked and sounded crazy. My freshly applied makeup was smeared already from the frustration tears. Part of his undigested breakfast was on the ends of my hair. I was not going to be able to cover all this up in the ten minutes before Toni came to work. As I was winding down my cursing and name-calling, I noticed that Dylan was lying on his bedroom floor, looking like death warmed over.

In the ten minutes, I was able to change my clothes, fix my face, and wipe the vomit out of my hair. By the time Toni came to work, there was not even a hint that our home was anything but love and light. I was even wearing a smile. It occurred to me, though, that Robbie and Claire left for school with this experience in the rearview mirror.

I worried about us all. This could not be good for any of us. Dylan just kept calling us names and blaming his dad and me for sending him away. Claire was getting more irritated the closer she got to university as she understood that we had eaten through the college funds. Now I was hearing the criticism in stereo. The more we pushed back on Dylan for his substance abuse, the more he berated us with obscenities that I had to look up in Urban Dictionary to decipher. He kept insisting his behavior was normal for a teenager.

I didn't know what normal was. Even though I knew my violent childhood was not normal, I didn't think the way my peers were raising children was normal either. I struggled to find the sweet spot between my childhood and the "give everyone a trophy" child-rearing. I couldn't figure out if everyone gets a trophy. How does a child know when they are actually doing well? How would they be inspired to work harder? I knew that falling down drunk at eight o'clock on a Thursday morning was not normal but couldn't figure out what is normal.

When Claire was filling out her wish list of classes for her eleventh-grade year, I had informed her that she would be going to the community college, and we could use that to her advantage. She could use this time to take a class that she is interested in but is concerned that she wouldn't get an A. She could use the opportunity to stretch herself because she wouldn't have to qualify for a four-year school out of high school. She chose physics. Claire is objectively beautiful; she had been scouted twice by modeling agents. She had options that are not available to the rest of us plain people. I was proud and surprised she chose physics.

The first day of her physics class, she came home from school. It was three in the afternoon, so I was working. "Mom, you have to help me get out of the physics class. Michelle says I am not smart enough."

Anger was so accessible for me at this point that I went from level 5 to 10 in an instant. "What the heck! Who is Michelle to say something like that?" I knew Michelle was a good student, but what kind of chutzpah do you need to say something like that? "She's just jealous 'cause she looks like a troll and she doesn't think you can be pretty and smart at the same time."

Claire was laughing because Michelle was conscientious of her looks and I was being a mean girl. "Mom, what if I don't have enough math to do the class? I am missing one of the math classes."

"Yep, you might not do well. That's why you did this. Remember this was to let you explore something you are interested in because you don't have to get an A." She nodded. "I'll help you if you still want to transfer out next quarter. Do one quarter."

She got an A and continued to take every physics class at the high school and, later, at the community college and eventually earned a scholarship.

I was counting the days to Dylan's eighteenth birthday to give him a set of luggage. In the meantime, I started regularly attending a meditation group to manage my own sanity. I kept up with the yoga and hiking in an effort to burn off the stress.

Zany Days

Dylan was spending most of the summer nights with Kyle and friends in Kyle's home. Kyle's mom, Debbi, seemed nice enough. She had driven Dylan home occasionally when he had drank too much and she didn't want to clean up the mess. As a single mother, a middle manager in a small company, she worked long hours. I knew that she was in the home with her boyfriend in the evenings. Dylan was showing up for work, so I felt comfortable overlooking the drinking. I found myself in the negotiating position frequently. Keeping peace in the home was important.

During one of our occasional morning jaunts to breakfast, Dylan informed me that Kyle had a problem with cocaine. He told me that Kyle had done cocaine every day for two months. Of course, Dylan denied using cocaine himself but tested positive for the drug three days later. His feigned surprise was laughable. He explained that they must have laced the weed he smoked the night before with cocaine.

I gave him three more days to *study* for another test, but even with the opportunity to clean up his act, he still failed the test. This was the last test. We stopped wasting our money because he was seventeen years old. We were still legally required to feed and clothe him even though he had no regard for the rules of the home. We had no control, but we still had full legal responsibility if he wrecked the car or committed a crime.

In my usual take-charge way, I e-mailed my Senator, Nancy Pelosi. As I am writing this, I know it is crazy, but I was so powerless and frustrated that I was responsible for this person with no recourse other than for him to become an emancipated minor which required his cooperation. My hands were tied. Of course, the e-mail went unanswered. Craig built a bedroom for Dylan in the garage with a space heater to minimize the impact to Robbie.

Dylan refused to sleep in the garage bedroom with sincere promises to stop cocaine, which coincided with his lack of money. He had used all his money, including his savings. Hope is seductive. We wanted the happy Christmas-card family and kept thinking these were bumps in the road that we could get over. Maybe if we told him we love him enough or gave him enough chances, he would realize how destructive his behavior is to the family and himself.

Now that we were through the cocaine phase, we could move forward with his education. He was nearing his eighteenth birthday with a lot of discussion regarding his future. He could stay in the home if he took classes at the local community college, which is less than one mile from our home, or he could go live on his own. He fed our hopes by making gestures toward signing up for school. Again, he was back to talking about his plan to be a police officer.

His behavior waffled between contrite and volatile. We watched TV together while I was working, but I refused to let him drive me anywhere. He would take advantage of the power position behind the wheel and drive aggressively in an attempt to intimidate me. A trip to Trader Joe's would turn into a screaming match. His point of view was understandable. In his view, we were abusing our power. It wasn't fair that he was too young and had too little power to live on his own and was dependent on us for his needs. In his mind, he had a right to do whatever he wanted to do with his own body. It is true that almost all conflict was started by my reaction to his self-destructive behavior. If I would just leave him alone, we would be able to live peacefully.

Accepting the possibility that I could be wrong in my determination, I tried it his way. I ignored the drunken arguments that he and Jillian had in his room. I ignored the use of hash in the garage. His use was prolific without my constant interference. The home was not more peaceful. The constant roller coaster of emotions fueled by the chemical cocktails did not foster serenity. In fact, it was more like the Wild, Wild West. When I would call Robbie or Claire on the carpet for bad behavior, they would tell me, "I am not on cocaine." This was all exacerbated by the reality that Craig and I could not get on the same page. It is difficult to get on the same page when there is no right answer. These problems are not problems we are supposed to have.

My thoughts changed one Tuesday afternoon watching Bill Burr, our favorite comedian. I was working on a file and Dylan was sitting in the bucket chair in the corner of my room. We had seen the hour-long special before but were laughing like we had never seen it before. I looked over at him sitting in the scoop chair with happiness. We still found common ground. He looked drowsy, but that could have been the hash he had smoked in the garage a few minutes prior.

Burr was explaining, "To me, this is not yelling. I am not yelling. I am passionate about my opinions, and I want to tell you all of them before you start talking again." I was laughing because this is exactly my modus operandi. Looking over at Dylan for affirmation, I noticed that Dylan was sleeping, but his neck was crooked in an unnatural position.

"That's so me, but I think it is you too. Don't you think?" For a second, I was denying the reality. He was nonresponsive. "Dylan, are you awake?"

Saying a prayer, walking over to the chair, I touched his cheek. His jaw was slack, and his eyes were rolled back when I lifted the lids. His lips had a faint blue tint, and I couldn't feel an active pulse. Lifting out of my own body, I watched myself, in increments of nanoseconds, hit him in the chest with my palm to startle him. It worked. His eyes opened and he said something with unintelligible speech.

I looked down and noticed he had urinated. "What did you take?" Digging through his pockets, I found four oblong pills with the identifier Xanax. His head dropped to the side, and I called 911. As the paramedics were in my room, Burr was ranting about women in his sarcastic over the top self-deprecating humor. I couldn't find the remote control, so it was the soundtrack to a terrible episode in our lives.

The ambulance left with a few of our new neighbors standing outside, seeing my shameful reality. I could be working and turning a file in three days early to my customers' delight and sharing a laugh with one of my favorite people. Instead, I would get yet another $1,500 medical bill from the ambulance not paid for by my insurance and a whole new set of fears. The hospital kept him long enough to flush his system with fluids and a stern warning.

We learned that he had been taking Xanax regularly. I had never heard of the drug, but it didn't look fun. It scared me that he could take a drug while I am in the room that could kill him. I had no control over him. It occurred to me that he could die while hiding the drugs. I worried that Robbie could wake up for school in the morning to his dead brother. We had a "coming to Jesus" discussion regarding transparency. We were not suggesting that we approved of his behavior, but we needed to know what he was doing so that we could protect him from himself.

He overdosed on Xanax again a week later. This time, I knew what I was looking at when he stumbled into the room with urine running down his pant leg. His pants were on backward. Craig was home this time, so he could take him to the hospital and save the $1,500 for the ambulance. I, like I had done this a hundred times, called the homeowner, waiting to have their home appraised and rescheduled the appointment. I finished my work and put dinner on the table. It was my thought that if I kept things normal that the impact would be lessened.

I learned this from my dad's mother. She was married to my grandfather for sixty years. He was an alcoholic, and because she was a woman before women's rights, she did the only thing she could do. She made dinner. Monday was meat loaf night and Tuesday was spaghetti night and so on. My father talked about this frequently, and when my grandma came to visit, she would make the spaghetti. I couldn't understand the excitement my dad had for this tradition until these Xanax moments.

I understood her efforts, and I was regretful that when I was fifteen years old, I protested going to eat my grandmother's spaghetti. I didn't like it, and the grease gave me a stomachache. It was the last time she would make the meal, and in retrospect, I am grateful my dad won the argument. My spaghetti dish was a baked rosemary chicken with little potatoes and carrots cooked in the bottom of the clay pot with the chicken drippings.

This new drug was inexpensive, easy to get, easy to hide, and had no smell. Meanwhile, my world was getting smaller and smaller. I went to church, but I worked in my home. My social interactions were limited to the hour-long church services and yoga classes. Both are places where silence is required. I didn't know how to talk to people. I didn't know how to answer the question, "How are you doing?" If I told the truth, I might start crying in public. I wasn't sure I would be able to stop. I was not certain this wasn't my fault.

This was so far away from what I thought my life would look like when I had children. I thought I would be a mother of three children that went to school and came home to do homework. I would have regular problems at the dinner table. In my imagination, they would not like my cooking and I would struggle to get them to eat their vegetables.

I Have a Way with Animals

The summer after Dylan turned eighteen years old, he moved to Isla Vista in southern California with friends. Isla Vista is the small town near Santa Barbara University. The entire town is filled with college-age students in various forms of clothing options. Bathing suits were considered fully dressed and day drinking was acceptable. Even with these loose behavior standards, Dylan was still cited with public intoxication twice in the first week.

The phone calls home were filled with tales of drunken excursions, but no job opportunities. This was the first time in two years that we had relief from his chaos. I knew that I lived in a pressure cooker, but I was unaware of the effect on me. It took a couple of days to stop waking up defensively. No longer was I waking up at 6:00 am to Dylan banging on our bedroom door to take his shower. I knew that it bothered me to get up and allow him into our space to take a shower, but I never considered that the effort to enforce the boundary would be worth the argument. I knew how to establish the personal space; all I needed to do was follow the kid's example. They were clear in their privacy standards.

Within a week, I was spontaneously smiling and randomly dancing. The only other experience I had like this was hiking the Grand Canyon with a thirty-pound back-pack and struggling the entire ten miles down the Kaibob trail with the weight. The weight distribution made bal-ance difficult; my body wanted to fall backward. When I removed the backpack, I felt so light that I thought I could fly. Every step and motion was so much easier.

Every part of my day was easier without the constant conflict; even the quality of my work improved. I knew that when I made dinner that it would be eaten by the four of us in peace. The four of us all hoped that this could be a new phase in our family. According to the phone calls home, the feelings were mutual. Dylan was also relieved to be free from our criticism of his behavior. The tickets for public intoxication were absorbing all his savings. His job search was halted, and he was running out of money. He was honing his manipulation skills while asking for money. The blaming and excuse making was tiresome. The more he called, the more clearly I could see the impact of his addiction.

One frantic Saturday-evening phone call home drove this point home. "Mom, I need my medical card number."

"What happened to your card?" I paused the movie the kids and I were watching on my bed. "Wait a minute while I get my wallet. Why do you need the card? What's wrong?"

I could barely understand him and had to ask him to repeat himself three times before I could understand. "I was petting a raccoon on the back porch. You would love it. We feed her and her babies. They are so cute, Mom.

Sean told me not to pet them, but I told him I have a way with animals. Then she bit me."

He did not think our laughter was supportive while he was scared he was going to die from rabies. No one in his immediate vicinity could drive as they were all intoxicated. Every time someone else walked in the room, I told them the story and everyone laughed again. Dylan was dejected by the growing laughter and was quoting the effects of rabies as reported by Wikipedia, but we couldn't understand him on the first try. "I need some money too so I can take an Uber, or should I have an ambulance come? I need to get to the hospital, and I am hungry."

He knew the magic words. I didn't want to pay for another ambulance and I wanted to go back to watching the movie. I sent him $25 so that I could get back to my movie, but it wasn't enough for him. "How many bars of Xanax did you take and when?"

Frequently, he forgot to lie when intoxicated. "Two a couple of hours ago. It's cheap here."

The movie was interrupted several times with phone calls which vacillated between "I love you" and "You're the worst mother ever. You don't care that I am dying." The kids were irritated that I had picked the movie and then missed the movie because I "always put Dylan first."

He would not answer the phone the following morning. Intellectually, I knew that he was sleeping off the party, but there was another part of me that worried that I should have done more. At some point in the flurry of phone calls the night before, I told him to put a Band-Aid on it and go to bed. Maybe I should have told him to call 911 and forget about the bill. It is absurd that ambulance trips aren't covered by my insurance. I was distracted during church with the certain knowledge that he was foaming at the mouth, lying on the couch in his friend's home.

When I finally heard from him the following evening, looking for money, he chastised me for calling him sixteen times. He told me he was a grown-up and could handle himself like a man. I knew the money I sent him was probably for buying intoxicants, but I wanted to keep him out of the house a few more days so I could finish watching a movie with the kids. I wasn't ready to put my backpack on again. I hoped he was buying food and gas with the money, but I was sure he was buying beer. At least beer has calories whereas the pills do not. I worried about his weight.

His roommate called once to tell me that Dylan had taken too much Xanax and fell asleep in the shower. He was worried that any friction between him and Dylan would affect his relationship with our family. His roommate was a family friend for years, but Dylan's behavior was testing the friendship. Dylan was the only nonstudent in the home during finals. His disruption was making it hard for them to study.

I wasn't surprised when I turned my phone back on after church the following Sunday to find several messages from Dylan asking for gas money. He had to come back home because his roommates had threatened to cut his throat. As I was putting my metaphoric backpack on, I felt validated. Even his peers found his behavior unacceptable, and he had been there a total of nineteen days. Our family had been doing this for a total of five years.

I made a commitment to myself. I didn't know how it would look or where to start, but I was going to commit to myself as much as I was committed to the people in my family. I was beginning to understand that I never included my needs in the decision-making. I kept telling myself that when the kids are grown, I would get to be a person. Craig and I also decided that we were going to open up a space for Dylan to be honest about his drug use without judgments. Maybe Mr. Aloo, his high school guidance counselor, was right when he suggested that I look at the drug addiction as though it was a problem that we could conquer together instead of being adversarial. We worried that he would die while we were avoiding the truth. We made it clear that we did not approve of his drug use, but we could all stop pretending.

Dylan used this option when it suited him, but Robbie and Claire took advantage of this open line of communication. They felt free to ask me questions and talk about things I would never talk about with my parents. I became the trusted adult in the room.

No One Is Safe

When he came home from Isla Vista, Keith was happy to have him back at work. Working with Keith kept him on a regular schedule and gave him a reason to be home in bed in the evenings. They picked up their conversation where they left off, talking about politics constantly while working in the yards of the wealthy. While he was wandering around the vineyards with successful and interesting men and women, a whole new world opened up in front of him. It was the first time he understood the financial limitations of our family. We had never taken a European vacation or hiked the Inca Trails in Peru. We worked seven days a week most of the year.

It was my hope that this would inspire him to work toward this end, but he was angry that we had not attained this success. This was a direct affront to me because I was proud of the fact that I had pulled myself out of the track I was on as an active alcoholic. Every morning, I said a prayer of gratitude that our family ran a business that put food on our table even through the recession in a profession that was hit so hard by legislation. His comments were hurtful and shaming, but we kept reminding ourselves that his comments were born in ignorance.

His views on life were both naive and cynical at the same time. He was naive about himself; he kept telling us that he could quit his drug use whenever he wanted and we were overreacting. His most frequent accusation was that we were jealous and just didn't want him to have fun because we weren't having fun. He would frequently remind us that we made getting sober look terrible.

In truth, I had to admit that I thought my life would look different after twenty years of sobriety. The irony was not lost on me. He was criticizing me for being miserable as he was causing chaos in the home. Craig and I stopped talking about the drug use at some point and focused more on the kids that were doing what they were supposed to be doing.

Claire and Robbie were more mature than their peers. This was evidenced one day when I was crying in my room after a heated argument with Dylan and Craig. I was beside myself. The argument was two against one; Craig and Dylan were insisting that we should have guns in the house. I had grown up with guns and understood that some households could manage guns safely. I didn't think that was our reality, but Craig forever lived in hope. He wanted to divert Dylan's focus with something exciting, like hunting deer and rabbits. I lost the argument. Without my asking, Claire silently came in the bedroom and set a cup of Earl Grey tea on my nightstand and left without a word.

As angry as I was about losing the argument, I valued Craig's ability to stay hopeful. Dylan did have weeks of minimal drug use, which were peaceful days. We loved watching comedians and TED talks. We had long talks during our hikes on the local trails. He learned to play the ukulele and drove us crazy playing it for hours on end. After mastering the ukulele, he bought a guitar at a garage sale and learned several Bob Dylan songs, singing them constantly. I thought we were moving out of a bad phase in our family, and then Kyle started showing up again.

Cocaine and psychedelics were prominent features in our lives again. If he kept his behavior to himself, I could ignore the drug use, but living with him was an emotional roller coaster every day.

I didn't hear Dylan come home one afternoon until he burst into my office where I was working and started yelling, "Why are you so cheap that you won't get us iPhones? Even homeless people have iPhones, but you are such a control freak you won't spend the money."

I didn't even look up to address him. "No, I won't spend the money. You have a job. Buy your own." Those were the magic words that made him pick up the board that kept my printer stable on the desk and started banging the bedpost.

"I could have been killed today because I didn't have an iPhone." He threw the board at Craig's computer and shattered the screen.

This was too familiar. I grew up with the random acts of violence; he crossed the line once too often. I couldn't do this again. Craig was on his way home, so I gave him a heads-up before he walked in the door. Craig threatened, "I am going to beat his ass when I get home." Dylan could hear the threat and grabbed a tire iron and was waiting for Craig when he got home.

He was standing at the top of the stairs when Craig walked up, and just like being in a movie, Robbie grabbed the tire iron when it was lifted to strike and broke the momentum on the way down. When Craig lifted his hand to protect himself, the iron broke his finger. Dylan ran out of the house with the iron in his hand. Love is weird. After all this, we worried about him as he ran out of the house, he was still our son.

After we dealt with the police and emergency workers, we went looking for him. We found the tire iron in a bush two hundred feet from our house, next to his vomit. He came home remorseful. Craig held him while he cried and explained that he had been held up at gunpoint and had no cell service to call for help. Never mind that he was held up by a former classmate while buying cocaine in the local park.

He spent a lot of time in his shared room on his computer in the deep web, looking at inhumane content. He wasn't showing Robbie the content, but the room is small and overseeing, and hearing could not be avoided. Robbie was fourteen years old being exposed to beheadings and murder porn. Dylan repeated what he heard on these sites; it freaked everyone out when he talked about people eating human flesh. Robbie started sleeping downstairs in the living room, and Claire was living with her boyfriend. We all knew that we needed to come up with a different solution but were scared to kick him out as if it were throwing him away.

I thought about sending him to a therapist but decided that our time and money would be better spent on Craig and me in marriage counseling. Maybe we could find a way to get on the same page. When I was interviewing people on the phone, I listened to their voice for strength although I wasn't sure how I would know strength. It seems that picking a therapist is a crapshoot. I have been to therapists crazier than me. I needed someone who had treated a superhero like me before. They needed to be able to keep up with my intellectual and spiritual prowess. I chose Josh, a middle-aged faithful Jewish man.

I requested that he be truthful and not pull any punches because I didn't have the money or time to waste. We were paying for this out of our own pockets as the insurance did not cover the expense. He did not hesitate to inform me in our first session that I was not a superhero and that I was a codependent to our son. To be fair, superheroes and codependents look very similar. Josh was an expert in the Imago format of counseling, which is an effective communication style. Craig and I never perfected it though. We argued both to and from the sessions. I did wake up to certain realities.

I was stuck in survival mode, but I wanted to live. My insides were evaporating, but the shell of me was still walking and talking. "Elvis has left the building." Envy dominated my life. I struggled listening to Dylan's friend's mom's talk about college expenses. I politely asked friends about their out-of-country vacations, asking pointed questions as if I would be making the trip in the following year. I brought my shoulds, becauses, and sorrys into therapy.

Every question Josh asked me was answered with an "I should" or "because I" or "I am sorry." I said "I am sorry" so often that I would say sorry for saying "I am sorry." Self-doubt absorbed my every moment.

I reluctantly started taking a pain medication with an opiate component to treat the nerve damage in my neck. I had been using chiropractors, massage therapists, and ibuprofen with limited results. I took so much ibuprofen that I was bruising with minor collisions and my digestion system was disturbed. My doctor was very careful with me. We used cortisone shots sparingly and as little medication as possible. Every month, I would have to negotiate with the pain because I was running low on medication before my next appointment.

I hid my pain medication and Robbie's ADHD medication in the gun safe. Although I was careful, I would run out before the prescription. One time, when I was counting the pills, I was distracted for a minute by a phone call when Dylan walked in. I was away from the bottle for less than a full minute, but Dylan managed to take four pills. Two days of medicine. He had two in his pocket, and Craig found two in his drawer. Before we could get the two from his pocket, he dry swallowed the two pills in front of us. Craig was frustrated that I had left my medication available. I should take better care.

I never took my medication with an open door again. Because I was so careful with the medication, I assumed that I was somehow doubling up on my dose occasionally. I never take enough medication that I got high, so I might not realize I had double dosed. There are no auto refills for class 1 drugs. When I ran out before I could get another prescription, my life came to a halt. Somehow, I still came up short but couldn't see the error of my ways. I counted Robbie's medication every day to make sure I wasn't double dosing his ADHD medication. I was sure I was going crazy when two of Robbie's pills and four of my pills were missing. I knew that I had not given him three pills in a morning. There were only two explanations, and both seemed unreasonable. Craig insisted that he had not been in the gun safe and Dylan did not have the entry code.

The strain was getting me. I was still going to counseling and practicing meditation, but maybe I was losing my mind. When I asked Dylan if he was in the safe, he confessed to taking a lot of pills. He never admitted to having the code but found the safe unlocked, which was possible. The fear was overwhelming. I had spent so much of my childhood not being safe, and here I was again as an adult feeling unsafe. Not only did he have access to the medications that we needed for his pleasure, he also had access to the guns. I was not smart enough to keep us safe. He was smarter than me, and I was losing the war. I was going to have to admit defeat in order to shore up the borders.

Answer the Phone

"Mom, this place is terrible." Dylan was waking up to his reality. "You tricked me. I know you hate me."

"No, I didn't trick you." I was barely awake at 5:00 a.m. This rehab must let them keep their phones. "Can I call you back? I haven't had my coffee yet. When are you in group? I'll call you back. I promise."

I made arrangements for a rehab in Astoria, Oregon, and purchased the airline ticket. I made sure the kids were out of the house when I confronted Dylan with the choice of rehab or living in his car. I still felt the sting of guilt about my methods of getting Robbie out of the house. Robbie had asked for a note excusing his planned absence that morning but did not like the note I wrote.

"Mom, I cannot hand this note into the attendance office." He was shoving it back in my hand. "You are not funny."

I grinned in spite of myself. "I think I am hilarious, and this is the note you get. So you should go to school before you have more Saturday school."

"I am so tired. Please, Grace said I could sleep at her house today while her parents are at work and she has Pizza Rolls in her freezer." The circles under his eyes were dark purple. I knew he was exhausted, but I needed him to be gone, and I was sure that he never let me excuse him for the day because he had *explosive diarrhea*.

Craig grabbed the note. "You should go to school, Robbie. Doesn't the cute girl work in the attendance office? I would never hand this note to her. Your mom is evil." He forgot his sweatshirt, but he went to school. He would sleep well tonight.

Dylan started with insults and threats and moved to pleas for compassion. Craig, always compassionate, was on team Dylan. I was in the triangle yet again. I informed them that either Dylan was leaving the home or I was. I was not going to spend one more night under the same roof.

I was hysterical in my presentation. I had no control over my emotions, but this time, it worked in my favor. The element of surprise also worked. Sun Tzu's *The Art of War* states appear where you are unexpected. I wanted him to get on the plane. If he didn't get on the plane, he would end up homeless on my back porch. After much conversation with the rehab center, he chose to get on the plane because he was terrified of being homeless.

His phone calls home from rehab were laced with profanity and blame. He called ten to fifteen times a day to plead with me for another chance and curse me when denied. He complained constantly about the conditions of the facility, and yet when he butt dialed me two weeks into his stay, he sounded like he was having a good time. I listened to him for approximately twenty minutes; they were playing spades. He stayed for two and half months before he used his way out of the program with two men I didn't know and his new friend Justin.

I didn't know where he was for twenty-four hours. Because he was an adult, I had no access to his medical records. My phone calls were going unanswered, and the hospital can't even tell me if he is still admitted. They could call me for payment, and they did frequently. I was so relieved to hear from him that I forgot to be mad.

"Mom, I screwed up." I was crying when he called the office line. "I was going to the store with my friends, and one of them stole a bottle."

"So you are not sober?" I sat in self-hatred at my desk. Why was I sniveling? "Can you get back into the program?"

"Is that all you care about?" His anger, so familiar, snapped me back. "I had to stay in my car last night and I am hungry and you are just focused on my sobriety."

"Well, yeah." The recovery times became quicker and quicker the longer I lived in the chaos—from tears to She-Woman Warrior in the blink of an eye. "That's what you are doing there. I am giving you a chance to take your head out of your butt and find your life. I can't make you take the opportunity. I can only give you the opportunity."

His adversarial behavior prevented him from getting a second chance that is sometimes granted for a slip while in the second phase of the program. He was causing havoc in the facility with his rants during group times. His favorites were "This thing is a cult" and "Rehabs are a scam." When I called the facility to talk about his being given a second chance, they said they would be able to put him into a facility in Texas, but he couldn't stay there. He was too disruptive.

"Mom, where were you? I have been calling the office phone for hours." He was barely controlling his agitation, which meant that he wanted something.

"Sorry, I was in a yoga class. What's up?"

"I know why you sent me to rehab. I promise if I get to come home, I'll only drink a few beers a night and sometimes I'll smoke some weed." He was currently homeless in his car with Justin, one of the heroin addicts he shared a room with in the program.

"Dylan, we have tried that plan for two years, and you haven't managed to make that happen."

Justin was tall, dark, and handsome. Girls flocked to him even in his homeless state. They lived off the kindness of these women. I called Dylan every day but did not send money. I ordered pizza to make sure he was eating. Dylan was good about answering the phone until, one day, he didn't and I unraveled. I had been checking in on him every few hours, keeping a record of where he was parked and who he was with.

The phrase *sick with worry* became real for me. Each hour without an answer was agony. Every action in the day was coated thick with worry. My arms were heavy, and I had to force my body to move, like I was a marionette. It looked like I was working and making dinner, but not really. Craig, Robbie, and Claire were understandably tired of hearing about Dylan, so I was in my worry alone. Sleep was sporadic with occasional unanswered phone calls. I was full of self-doubt. Could I be wrong? Shouldn't I let him come home? He was my son. What kind of mom leaves her son homeless? Maybe Al-Anon is wrong.

In the morning, I was loopy with distress when I called the nonemergency police number and described my son and his car. The police officer clearly had conversations like this before. He was both professional and kind. I told him that Dylan had been in the Safeway parking lot the day before. Within ten minutes of my conversation with the police, Dylan called me, saying, "Don't call the cops on me." I was grateful to hear his voice even if he was scolding me for my crazy-mom behavior. I reflected his frustration with; "Then answer your stupid phone."

Doris, my meditation teacher, kept telling me, "Stand as presence." I went to a meditation group that Doris held in her home every other Tuesday. Her small perfect home always smelled good when we came in. She cooked a vegetarian meal that we shared after a lengthy guided meditation. Initially, I couldn't sit for five minutes without moving and looking around. It took me almost a year before I could sit quietly for forty-five minutes.

The meditation practice was becoming an integral part of my mental health, but when she would tell me to stand as presence, I had no clue what she was talking about. Every time she said it, I would try to figure out what she meant. I asked her to define the words in the sentence.

"Could you define *presence* please?" Maybe I could trick her into accidently telling me.

Her voice was ever assured. "You will know when you are ready." This drove me buggy.

I kept coming because I loved sitting at her small table with my friends, eating delicious food I didn't cook and riding to and from with Frank. Frank is quick-witted, well-read, and has an infectious laugh. Maybe I would know when the time came and maybe all that happened was having dinner with awesome people.

Social Security

"Mom, I am hungry. My food stamps are gone." He was still homeless in his car. "I am tired of pizza. Could you call in a sandwich?"

"Didn't you just get your food stamps?" I was distracted by work. One of my files was late. "What kind of sandwich, and do you have the phone number?"

I interrupted the phone number to ask again, "What happened to the food stamps?"

"I used part of them and then sold the rest for beer." He couldn't see me shaking my head.

"Okay, I am running out of money, so I can't do this often. You can pick up your sandwich in twenty minutes. Please be careful. I called the Craigslist posting about the room, and they already filled the space, so you are going to have to keep looking." I hung up and called in his order.

I was stuck in limbo. Every pore of my being told me to stop the charade and bring Dylan home, but I had Robbie and Claire who were flourishing. Claire was getting straight As with her primary focus on physics and advanced mathematics. Robbie was able to randomly bring his friends home with no concerns over his older brother's inappropriate behavior that would discourage return visits. I was aware that I didn't have the ability to keep Dylan safe in my home anyway. He had overdosed in my home four times, twice while I was in the room with him. However, I had all this energy in my hands, I had to do something.

I had an idea while I was walking by a homeless man that I knew lived in the neighborhood. If I couldn't take care of my son, maybe I could take care of someone else's son. It could be a weird kind of social security. I needed people to be generous with my son even when I couldn't. I already served two organizations in my community faithfully. One organization provided permanent housing and one provided canned foods and other services, but I started paying attention to the individuals who lived on the streets in my neighborhood.

There was a man who spends his days in front of 7-Eleven. I have never seen him intoxicated, and he liked Jack. Jack liked licking the crud off his face. I still don't know the gentleman's name, and he doesn't know mine, but every day I walked down to 7-Eleven and checked in on him. If he wasn't there, another man who walked the neighborhood with his dog, Lucky, in a baby stroller benefitted from a meal. There is never a shortage of opportunities. They started to get to know me.

As I was walking around town, doing my errands, homeless men and women addressed me with salutations and smiles. I was becoming one of them. On occasion, they would offer to share their treasures. A gentleman on a Sunday morning offered me a drink of vodka. Besides the fact that I was on my way to church, this wasn't my fantasy of breaking my sobriety. If I were going to break my sobriety, it would be with expensive champagne in a fancy restaurant.

He asked, "Are you sure? It's the good stuff. Smirnoff." As I politely declined, impressed by their generosity, another man popped up out of nowhere.

I could smell him before I could see him. "Do you want a connector?" I looked down at his hand to find a small cylinder piece of plastic.

Having worked in an ICU of a psychiatric hospital for eight years in my 20's, I knew that I was going to get a moment of entertainment, and it was my job to be respectful. "What does the connector do?"

He explained, "It helps me to talk to the aliens."

"Awesome. That's nice, but I already have one." When the hospital I worked in closed down due to lack of funding more than fifteen years ago, the patients were dumped onto the streets with no follow-up care. "Can I get you a burger and fries?"

He looked offended by my offer. "No, why do you ask?"

Being quick with a cover story is the name of the game. "I was going to lunch and just wanted to include you." Obviously, not a good cover story. It was 8:00 a.m. on a Sunday morning.

"That's nice, but I already ate." We said our goodbyes, and I went to church.

I was standing in line in McDonald's one day to get Robbie's food when I noticed the man behind me was one of my regulars. After I ordered my meal, I told the cashier that I would pay for the gentleman behind me. The man cracked a smile and told me, "Not today. I am good today." Apparently, there is a code in this community. They only asked for what they needed. I had watched these folks share the cigarettes I bought them. I watched the healthy defend the more vulnerable against the aggressive. My hope was that the community that Dylan was living in was as cohesive as this group in my little city.

Maybe this is what God is—a system similar to gravity. I could slip into or out of this system of love any time I wanted. It seemed reasonable that God isn't an entity but rather an energy that could be accessed when I chose.

"Mom, you finally got a cell phone." He was calling me on the way to the gym. "You are the last person on earth to have a cell phone."

"I know. I was trying to control the effect the business has on me." I was panting, almost running. "Everywhere we go, I get at least two phone calls from business no matter the time of day. I wanted the ability to focus on my family when I was with my family and not be working 24-7."

"I can tell you can't talk, so I'll just tell you that Justin and I found a place. We have to share a room, but no big deals." He sounded almost happy. "I can't work at the gas station in the rain and then sleep in my car in the rain."

"Wow! That's great." I looked at the time. "Could I call you back later? I love you." I started running to get to my class.

Where's the Bottom?

"Dylan, Dad and I decided that you should stay in Oregon for Christmas. It will probably be too hard for you to leave our home again." This was a conversation that I mentally prepared for. "We rented a home in Astoria for three days. We'll bring a little Christmas tree and we'll go to church up there."

"Can you bring Jack?" I felt the pull. "I miss Jack. Can Justin stay with us too?"

"Sure, I would like to meet him. I'll make a stocking for him too." This went smoother than I expected. I expected a rant about my controlling behavior.

"I got a new job at Sahara Pizza!" he continued. "There is a cute girl that works there."

"Honey, I am so happy for you. I am proud of you. You are picking yourself up by your bootstraps. Good on you. I have to go back to work. I love you."

The home that Dylan and Justin were living in was a traditional Victorian home with four bedroom and three bathrooms. The pizza parlor that Dylan was working at is the same place I ordered pizzas from while he was homeless. He sounded like he was having fun and making friends. There were a few bumps, but he was supporting himself and getting to know girls. I still called every day to check in with him. I knew he was drinking every day, and his speech was slurred sometimes early in the morning. I assumed that pills were still in the picture.

We had considered bringing Dylan home for Christmas but decided we would like to see Astoria. If things weren't going well, we could leave early if we drive, but if we flew Dylan down to the Bay Area, it might be harder to end the experience early. He seemed to be getting over his home-sick days and didn't need to stir the longing for home. We packed the tree, presents, and decorations in the Ford Explorer and headed north. I was excited to see Dylan; it had been six months. Astoria is rainy and gray. We were on our way to the little Episcopal Church down the street for Christmas day services but were sidetracked when we went to his house.

His four roommates were not home when we arrived. The kitchen was filthy with rotting food on the counter, and the floor was sticky with grime. The garbage was over-flowing, and the food in the refrigerator was moldy. His room didn't look better. There were beer bottles sitting in the room that Justin had urinated into and left to clean up another day. The bathroom was unusable because the toilet had not been cleaned in months, and there was dried vomit on the seat. We spent Christmas morning cleaning the home in our Sunday best.

I couldn't figure out if there is a lack of shame or if this was manipulative. He knew we were coming and didn't clean up for a reason. Either he was so intoxicated he couldn't or he left the mess to make us feel sorry for him and bring him home. He knew this would bother me and yet didn't hesitate to invite us in with no warning or explanation. He was surprised that I was disgusted and even grew frustrated that I was cleaning. Claire jumped right in with a garbage bag.

Dylan wasn't tidy, but historically he wasn't filthy. I wondered if we were looking at his bottom or if he was living in someone else's bottom. The rest of Christmas was spent in our rented cabin, eating, playing spades, and walking around Astoria. Astoria is a small town on the Pacific coast near the Washington state line. The view from his bedroom window looked at the bridge across the Columbia River. The traditional homes are not necessarily well maintained. The locals love to tell visitors that the movies; *Goonies, Short Circuit,* and *Kindergarten Cop* were made in Astoria in the late 1980s and early 1990s. There were statues and references to Louis and Clark in the parks and downtown areas.

Dylan was intoxicated most of the time that we were with him. His excuse was that he was nervous and needed "something to take the edge off." He was nodding off during Christmas dinner. When I asked if he was all right, he insisted he was just tired. Of course, when I called attention to his condition, the situation was made worse.

Claire told me, "Mom, stop!" She was frustrated because she had forecasted this exact situation in the car ride up Highway 5. She gave up Christmas with her boyfriend to spend it with us.

After several hours of cleaning Dylan's home and on our way back to our cabin, Claire's frustration was palpable. "I don't know why we are doing this. You are not going to make this better." Claire and Robbie had been on every bend and curve of this awful roller-coaster ride, except that they had less control than Craig and me.

Dylan had shared his alcohol with her when we got to the rental home. When I asked them to explain themselves, Dylan responded, "I just thought we could have a good Christmas."

Claire chimed in, "We're bonding. Isn't that what you wanted?" It was hard to argue with her because she was making the green beans to go with the cracked crab, and I didn't want her to stop helping me cook in this strange kitchen.

I went to bed early, and they stayed up playing games. Things didn't go well for them as evidenced by the Monopoly game pieces all over the floor and shot glasses lined up on the countertop.

As we drove home a day early, I prayed that we were looking at his bottom. During the recap in the car ride home, we all agreed that Justin was charming just as Dylan said he would be. He seemed to be the alpha male in their friendship. Dylan followed his suggestions without question. Justin wanted a ride to work three blocks down the street on Christmas Day. We were in the middle of a game of Pick and Tap and Dylan stood up in the middle of his turn and took him to work even though he was four deep into a six-pack of beer. The conversation ended when Robbie mentioned that Justin reminded him of Colin.

"Hi, Dylan, we're home now. This is just a quick call to say how much I love you and how much I loved seeing you. I wish you didn't drink so much." I could hear him sigh. "Do you work today?"

"No, I took the week off to be with you." Now it was my turn to sigh.

"How are you going to pay your rent if you take so much time off work?" I could hear the nag in my voice but had no ability to control it. "We were only there three days."

"I love you, Mom. I'll talk to you later." I was wrecking his high. His voice was drowsy.

Death by a Thousand Cuts

"Dylan, I have to talk to you seriously. Are you intoxicated right now?" I set aside twenty minutes to have a heart-to-heart with him.

"Mom, it's eight in the morning. Who do you think I am?" I could see his point, but he wasn't going to see mine, and I didn't want to argue.

"Sorry. You are right." I plunged forward. "Your dad and I are separating."

"What?" His confusion was understandable. "Why? You have been married like twenty-four years. Is this my fault?"

"No it's not your fault. You know Dad and I have struggled for years." He was crying as I continued, "Maybe we could be happy apart. We are going to still work together."

"Is it another man?" Also, a reasonable question.

"No. It's not another man, and in fact, if I do have another partner, it's not likely to be a man. It's likely to be a woman." I could hear the gasp.

"You are gay?" He was yelling.

"Well, I like both and I have tried to understand men for years and we just don't speak the same language." I was aware that I knew a lot about him, but he doesn't know that much about me. He knows me as his mom, not as a person. "Are you still there?"

"Okay. Do you have twenty bucks for gas?" That was easier than I expected. "I like this job, but I spend a lot of money in gas, and I don't get my paycheck for another three days."

"Sure. I'll send it through the checking account. Thanks for being so understanding. I love you."

The marriage had endured too much strain to continue on in a healthy way, so we separated after the Christmas in Astoria. Both of us had made every attempt to make the marriage work, but there were too many factors, and marriage counseling was too little too late. The expensive four-day marriage workshop only emphasized the abyss. I was jealous of other people's problems.

The workshop was in Monterey Hotel with an ocean view. The workshop absorbed the entire hotel, with fifty couples participating. The Israeli couple leading the retreat were married fifty-plus years and known for growing and perfecting the Imago method. They stood in the center of the room, demonstrating a communication technique, and then let us practice before they moved on to the next lesson. Most of the couples were empty nesters and, like us, have been married more than twenty years. Their troubles seemed dwarfed by ours. The wives talked about being ignored, and the men complained of being nagged. I didn't want their problems, but I didn't want mine either. I did not want to share our problems with the group and risk another incident like in the discovery program when I couldn't stop crying.

When it was our time in the center, I kept my arms close to my body because I could feel the sweat dripping down my rib cage. My voice was shaky, but I continued to speak my truth. I wanted to be considered in the marriage. An unintended consequence of focusing on Craig's health was that my needs sat in a position after Craig's needs and after the children. I felt that I was always getting the leftovers which isn't a lot.

The format of the exercise is to use "I feel" statements without interruption. The partner answers the "I feel" statements with "What I heard you say is," and then they repeat back the statements as they heard them and then asks the question "Did I get that right?" The first person reminds or clarifies missed statements or points. The listener asks, "Is there more?" Then the first person "crosses the bridge" to the listen to the other's "I feel" statements and the exercise continues.

I was scraping the surface in my "I feel" statements. The leader, sitting so close to me she could smell my nervous sweat, was prompting me to cut deeper. I was exposing my wounds of being ignored and the origin of these wounds from my crazy childhood. Despite my crippling fear of audiences, I was able to establish a boundary that I am not going to talk about the details of my childhood. I was light-headed during Craig's turn to give "I feel" statements.

He gave me the typical "I'm sorrys" for the gambling and buying a business without my consent. At some point in the marriage, he owned three bars, one of which I didn't even know existed for the first two weeks of ownership.

These apologies were not new to me, and in fact, I already forgave him for these infractions. I was talking about the minutiae in our days that kept a hostile environment. There were regular instances of challenging my parenting in front of the children. Even if I am wrong, which is frequent, it should be discussed in private.

Twenty minutes is not a long time when watching a movie, hiking, or doing yoga, but twenty minutes in front of forty-nine other couples with my personal wounds open on display was exhausting. The goal was to reduce the anger even if it was my fault; I just wanted to stop waking up angry every morning. My anger level when I woke up in the mornings was at a four out of ten and it could accelerate to a ten with the slightest provocation. We were both aware that our kids were the victims in our standoff but were powerless to change. Craig ended the conversation with the statement, "I don't know what you want me to do. I have Parkinson's."

He was right. I was the one changing the rules of the game in the middle of the game, but I didn't know what else to do. The twenty-five-year-old me that started this relationship had grown up in sobriety and motherhood. This was grossly unfair to both of us. The retreat didn't save the marriage, but it brought clarity.

The story I told myself was that I had bigger problems than the other retreat attendees, but my problems were exactly the same. It is the small things that ate us, like the way we say hello to each other or don't. The way I roll my eyes when he says something I deem ridiculous and the way I say his name. Once, when Dylan was four years old, he said his dad's name with the same pitch and cadence I use when I am annoyed with his father. It was like holding a mirror up in front of my face and I didn't like my reflection. I committed to being more respectful going forward in my interaction, but I failed.

Bone-tired, lying in the hotel bed after a shared meal with other couples, I watched this naked stranger, my husband, and wondered if I could do even one more day of marriage. I ran out of energy to be married, but I didn't know how to be single either. I was married before the internet. I only knew how to do one thing for a living, and that was running this shared business. We had to figure out how to keep the business running. The objective would be to run it peacefully when we couldn't do it while we were married. These were lofty goals, but it turns out that getting divorced is easier when you own nothing and the kids are almost grown.

Even though the marriage retreat did not save the marriage, it did help clarify my part in the conflict. Because it was my choice to end the marriage, I took the brunt of the social judgment. I was persona non grata for several months. It looks terrible to divorce a sick person. To confuse the matter more, I hadn't been talking to anyone but the marriage counselor and one hundred strangers in a workshop, about our marital problems, so it took everyone by surprise. I can pretend that I am private and discreet in an effort to be classy, but the truth is, I was trained in childhood to keep these things secret.

On the exterior, it looked like I left Craig because he was getting older and sicker. It is true that I had told him when we started the diagnosis process thirteen years prior that I would be either his wife or his nurse, but I couldn't be both. Initially, we both held firm in this boundary, but the last four years, I was everything—boss, nurse, wife, cook, mother; ad infinitum. Every morning, I woke up knowing I had one hundred tasks to complete in the next twenty-four hours and knowing there's only enough time and energy for fifty tasks. It was always about priorities, and I was low on the list.

When I thought about the "death till you part" thing I started to wonder more frequently about life spans. People lived a lot longer in modern times than they did when these vows were written. I didn't want to be married, wondering how long we were going to live, and the example we were giving our kids seemed irresponsible.

I was prepared for the societal reaction because I watched what happened to Debbie, Kyle's mom, when she left her sick husband after he was diagnosed with MS. She was treated like a pariah and lost almost all her friends. I was one of the people with my own criticism, especially when she started dating one of my friends; I was vocal in my opinions about marriage through sickness and health. Now, I was in the same position and hoped people were kinder in their judgments.

I didn't have the energy to explain myself to everyone as I was tempted. It made better sense to let my actions speak for themselves. I continued to be inclusive of Craig in our holiday celebrations and helped him with his medical needs, and we continued to go to the same church. It was easier to see his attributes when I didn't feel trapped. Craig is, at his core, generous and has a wicked sense of humor. It occurs to me that we both suffer from leash aggression. Once we were not tied to each other it got easier.

I was scared to throw my "seeing eye" person away though. Without having a full-time driver's license in the house, just getting groceries in the house was an effort. Claire had a driver's license but was busy getting straight As in the community college and working as a tutor. I had to learn basic skills with crippling self-doubt. Maybe, I was expecting too much from my life. Maybe, I was not meant to be happy. I wondered if I even wanted to be happy. As long as I was in chaos, I didn't have to be responsible for my actions; there was always an excuse.

There were issues I didn't even know I would have because I had taken Craig for granted in many ways. I have served as a commissioner for my city for more than a decade. One of the responsibilities is to wade through the crowd at the end of the free concerts and empty the garbage. Historically, I did this with Craig; I just followed him and didn't have to negotiate the crowd. It is hard for me to see in crowds, especially in the gray light of dusk. The noise wasn't helpful as I use my hearing to compensate for my vision. My first concert, I was embarrassed when I had a panic attack in front of another member. I had to explain my situation at the next meeting and ask to be paired with someone else at the concert.

Now, I wasn't waking up angry. I was waking up scared. The anxiety-filled self-doubt became a way of life, causing chronic diarrhea. I lost eighteen pounds in a few months; people were concerned I was anorexic because my weight dropped to ninety-seven pounds. As if the diarrhea wasn't enough, I had shingles on my torso. I wasn't starting single life off as a sexy beast. Gradually, people gathered around me and wrapped me in love. Even Craig was supportive. We became family and managed to work together better than we did when we were married.

"Mom, I just called to tell you how proud I am of you." He might have meant this and he might have been high, but I didn't care. I ate it up. "You are so brave."

"Thank you. I have someone on the other line. Are you okay?"

"Yeah, I just wanted to tell you I love you." He sounded like he meant it.

I told him, "I love you too. Thank you." I had to get back to my phone call before they hung up.

The Daffodil and the Condom

"Mom, why are you panting?" Now that I had a cell phone, I was always on someone's leash. It's good that it was Dylan on the other end of the leash.

"I am running today and swimming tomorrow." I stopped running.

"I just called you to tell you that I love you." I loved these phone calls.

"Did you need something?" I was aware that it was Friday morning and he might want money to start the weekend.

"Thirty bucks might be nice. I want to see the new *Spider-Man* movie." We both love movies.

"Promise me that you won't buy drugs with it. I heard the movie is going to be epic." I was getting cold as the wind was meeting my sweat. "I have to start running again because I am getting cold. I'll send it when I am done. It's only three miles today."

When Craig was diagnosed, I asked the neurologist if exercise was good for him or hurtful. I thought inviting oxygen into the equation with aerobics seemed like a good idea, but I could be wrong. Craig was in excellent shape for a man his age. I loved his body and didn't want to see that go away, but I was willing to follow the doctor's order.

She said, "The best thing for movement disorders is more movement."

My hands could not stop shaking and my insides were quivering, so I followed the doctor's order. I thought the best thing for my movement disorder was more movement. I started running three miles every day in an attempt to burn off excess energy. One of my favorite places to run is the community college around the pond because I don't have to compete with cars. There are duck families that have babies annually. The latest brood had eight babies. Their little fuzzy heads catch the sunlight as they are bobbing up and down while they learn to swim. On one of my runs, I noticed a daffodil unlike any I had ever seen; the inner cylinder was fringed. I took a picture of it and looked down to put my phone away when I noticed that I was standing on a used condom.

My initial reaction was disgust and a wonder about the logistics of this circumstance. Did they throw it out of the car window when they were done? Was this a homeless person making a good health decision? Then a God thought struck me. I was standing in the parking lot with the universe talking to me. It occurred to me that this was representative of my life's perspective. I frequently focused on the condoms instead of the daffodils. The daffodil was still there, and yet I was focused on the disgusting.

I thought about how many times people asked me how I was doing, and I would answer with a report of Dylan or Craig, not that they are disgusting all the time. I realized how I was functioning similarly in my business. I served the customers who were disrespectful first in order to prevent rejection. I spent a lot of time trying to satisfy the angry gods. I needed to change my perspective if I were going to get through this time in my life. I was going to have to stay focused on the daffodils.

The following week, I invited customers that had been disrespectful to use another company. As I focused on respectful customers, the business immediately made more money. I apologized to Robbie and Claire for my negligence. I committed to my happiness and went back to individual therapy. I didn't have the money for therapy, but I couldn't afford not to go to therapy.

I had grown accustomed to Josh during the couple's therapy, and he agreed to treat me as an individual with the caveat that he would not see us as a couple again. I needed his directness. He kept me focused on the daffodils despite my habitual focus on victimhood. Victimhood is enticing because I don't have to take personal responsibility. I was asking Dylan to take personal responsibility while I blamed the world for my circumstance. The problem is that I had legitimate reasons for blame, but I had to ask myself, "Do I want to be happy, or do I want to be right?"

Two years prior, my friends and I saw Desmond Tutu, the South African archbishop, at Grace Cathedral in San Francisco before he retired. He spoke at length about non-duality concepts during his sermon. I had never been in a room with such a powerful person. He is a small man, so we could not see him through the crowd when he came in the nave, but we could feel his energy. He greeted the congregation from the pulpit with the clucking of his native tongue. His message was, "I am human because you are human. I know how to talk and walk because you teach me. We need people to reflect our image, to tell us who we are." His words, spoken in his accent with his voice filled with joy, washed over me in baptism.

Years later, I talked about this with Josh. I grew up with the idea that I was defective and, therefore, not worthy. Using Desmond Tutu's truth, I could see that my mirrors were broken, which distorted my image of myself. It didn't make sense to tear open old wounds in my fragile state. We only addressed my childhood in general ways, just enough to understand my motivations and behavior. My childhood was like living in a fun house mirror exhibit at a carnival. The distorted images are not real, but my life decisions were based on these reflections.

The problem is that I haven't been a child in decades, but I was still choosing people who reflected the fun house image, thinking that the image is reality. I asked Josh every session, "Am I crazy?" He would answer me with the question, "What do you think?" until one day I was earnest in my request to answer the question. He finally answered, "No, you are not crazy." I had to ask the question several more times over many more sessions with his reassurance before I could finally trust his assessment.

Gradually, the diarrhea stopped and my anxiety subsided. Even though my business was doing better, it wasn't profitable. One Tuesday, I was sitting beside the fountain, waiting for my two o'clock therapy session, when Claire called to tell me the power was turned off. After calling in a payment and making a payment arrangement for the rest, I still went in with a check for my therapy. If I was going to disrupt the family with divorce, I better make it worth the trouble and stop the destructive cycle.

"Hi, Dylan." I was agitated. "The *Spider-Man* movie doesn't come out until next week. What did you use the money for?"

Defensively, he responded, "I put it in my gas tank and bought McDonald's." Because this was entirely possible, I let this be my truth.

"How are you doing?" My voice softened.

"I am always cold," he explained. "My house is cold because the landlord doesn't want a high energy bill and the heater in my car doesn't work and I get wet when I bring the pizzas to the door."

"Do you still have the nice jacket Dad gave you for Christmas?" I hate being cold and sympathized with this plight. I wished that this was different. I wished that I could bring him home and have him be an integral part of my household.

"Yeah, I am just tired. I have to go take Justin to work, so I have to go." I was surprised that he didn't ask for money or for me to solve his problem. He just told me, "I love you."

Hope Springs Eternal

"Mom, if I go to school, would you help me financially?" He sounded nervous. I better be careful in my response.

"I would love for you to go to school." I was trying not to give my power away by sounding too excited. "Do you have a school nearby?"

"There's a community college within walking distance." His voice was stronger.

"Wow! When can you sign up?" I was completely betraying myself at this point. I couldn't suppress the delight.

"I already signed up."

"For real? That's awesome!" I let three phone calls go by unanswered.

"Did you sign up for classes?" If he said yes, I was going to cry.

"I am taking a philosophy class and a photography class. The advisor told me to start slow. She was so nice, Mom." He was relieved that I was going to help him.

"I am so happy for you." He could not see the tears "You are going to love school. Your mind is your favorite playground. You watch Stanford lectures online as a hobby. Now you are going to get credit for the lectures. I love you, but I have to go. The phone call I have been ignoring is calling back for a third time. I love you so much."

All the years of bribing and cajoling him to go to school and it only took one rainy winter in Astoria to persuade him that he didn't want to spend his life working minimum wage jobs. Justin, still sharing a room with Dylan, was not supportive with this decision and bullied Dylan while he was studying. He turned up the music to make it difficult to concentrate. He told Dylan that he was wasting his time and became physically threatening. My concern for Dylan's physical safety grew every day.

A drunken brawl one night resulted in a dry spell for Dylan. He went to a few AA meetings and became an ardent student of philosophy. He called every day with freshly learned theories of Nietzsche, Marx, and Descartes. He was developing his own ideas of the inner workings of the world and his own mind. Dr. Johnson, his professor, was friendly with the students and would hold court in the bar with lectures off campus. He was overeducated for his position at a small community college with classes that max out at fifteen students, not because of prestige but lack of interest. His followers, though few, were faithful.

The more I talked with him about his classes, the more I had to control *The Want*. *The Want* is the powerful desire that is a physical phenomenon within me. It manifests first with a hollow in the back of my throat and continues on through my trunk and ultimately through my hands. *The Want* is the force that moves me forward from being the stinky kid in school wearing threadbare hand-me-downs to a respected member in my community. When *The Want* is undisciplined, though, it causes havoc. I watched Dylan playing with *The Want*. He was teasing it with words I have waited to hear for years. He talked about his meetings and his sponsor and his stupid mistakes.

We knew Dylan should move out of the room away from Justin but couldn't afford another expense after Christmas. We made a plan for Dylan to escape to the hotel down the street from his home in the event of violence. I was trying to buy time for another check from my big customer and needed to find an affordable option. He was paying his own rent, but I would need to supplement the rent if he was going to continue in school. As expected, the hysterical call came in the middle of the night.

"Mom, it happened." His voice was pressured, but he wasn't crying. "The hotel clerk needs your card number before he will let me go in the room."

"Give me a minute. I can't find my purse." I just fell asleep, so it was easy to wake up and read the numbers. "Okay, go upstairs, put your stuff in the room, and I'll call in a sandwich from the all-night diner down the street. When you get back, take a bath and watch a movie. I have to go back to bed. I have a lot of work in the morning."

The argument started with a discussion about the history of the United States in their room. Justin was drunk and Dylan was arrogant and pigheaded. Dylan made a remark that suggested that Justin is stupid, and Justin punched him in the face twice. He continued to throw him around the room, calling him a "pussy." Dylan called the police who broke the fight up and helped Dylan get to the hotel room. He stayed for three days in the run-down hotel while I made arrangements for another living situation. He went to meetings and continued to study while in the room.

The most affordable and available room was in a boarding home with older veterans. Dylan was the youngest resident by thirty years. Everyone had a room and shared a kitchen; every floor shared a bathroom. These old guys would sit in the courtyard with coffee cans for ashtrays in their plastic chairs that dried quickly after a rain. They would gather at the crack of dawn, smoking their first cigarette with a cup of Folgers coffee. They told the same five stories of their service in the military. All had one piece of clothing, noting the branch of armed services they served in decades prior. He was their new audience, and he loved their stories. At night, they would all be drunk on cheap beer. He started drinking with them but managed to still function. They loved him, and he was having fun in school.

He kept his part-time job, which wasn't enough to cover the rent and food. I agreed to pay the rent as long as he was in school. His drinking didn't appear to be interfering with school. He was getting straight As in classes, and he was excited for his future. His philosophy teacher inspired him, and his photography projects were fun.

I felt like we were out of the woods and I could focus on my own life as a single person and my finances. I found myself being lonely. My entire life had been focused on the family and their needs. My own needs took a back seat. There were a lot of people I served with on volunteer projects and I called friends, but no one that I could call when

I was falling apart on a Sunday afternoon. The only person I was talking to was Josh, but therapists are not substitutes for friends.

If I were going to make friends, I was going to have to let people see the underbelly of my life. I was so nervous reaching out to, Jennifer, a woman from church. I had to start telling people the truth without being a person who overshared and made the whole friendship about me and my troubles. Actually, there was no danger of oversharing. I only tell the necessary details and then move on to talk about movies, books, and politics. I was violating my family of origin's first rule: what happens here stays here.

When I was a kid, I told a friend what was happening in my home, and the friend went home and told her mom. Her mom approached my stepmom who freaked out, thinking she was going to go to jail for her behavior, and she made me go back to my friend's mom and tell her that I had lied. I felt stupid and learned my lesson. I wasn't a kid though. I could have friends that know my truth. I still couldn't get my mouth to stop drying up and my body to stop spontaneously breaking out in a sweat when I would talk about my shameful parts. I had a lot of shame about Dylan and my finances.

The truth is that I had access to more money than most of my friends but had my power was turned off three times in my first year of separation. I couldn't manage to keep the money after medical debts and the IRS back payments. I couldn't blame anyone else but myself and *The Want*. *The Want* was unchecked in 2005 when the business grossed almost half a million dollar in a year. I thought this would be forever and that I had finally arrived.

We were appraising mansions and determining values of homes that I never even knew existed. Sometimes, the homes belonged to famous people and CEOs of Fortune 500 companies. Envy swallowed me whole. I was living in a run-down three-bedroom home with one bathroom. *The Want* told me that I deserved a five-bedroom and three-bathroom home with a pool. We remodeled the home we were living in with abandon and no regard for money. When the world financial market melted, we were not prepared for our tax debt. As quickly as envy swallowed me whole, guilt was next.

Intellectually, I know that Dylan is an individual that makes decisions by himself, but I felt that if I had been a better mother, he would be able to make healthier decisions. If I had been financially responsible, we would have more options. When my friends would rebuff this notion, I would think they were nice liars. Sometimes, they would echo Josh without knowing it, which was helpful. I was hearing things in stereo. Of course, Dylan had leverage over me as long as I believed that I was, in part, responsible for his chaos.

"Hey, Mom." It was the third phone call of the day. "I am working on my photography project. I know you are walking to the gym, but can you help me with ideas?"

"What choices do you have?" This was fun.

"I can do the project on a couple of topics, but I am thinking about birth." It was six thirty in the evening, and his voice was clear as a bell.

"What about an egg?" I have never taken photography. I studied biosciences in my unfinished college career.

"Everybody does that. I need something original." I haven't done this since he was in the eighth grade, writing a poetry book.

"What about born-again Christians or AA, as in rebirth?" He sighed and hung up.

"Damn it. I am sorry. Why do I always have to push things? Things were going so good." But I was talking to a dial tone.

Can You Hear the Music?

"Hi, Mom. Why are you going to the gym later than usual?" His voice was blurred with an unknown substance. That is to say it was unknown to me.

"I am going to Zumba." I was trying to beat the rain.

"Have you started dating anyone?" The question took me by surprise but was an indication that he was getting used to the idea of my marital status.

"No. I went on a few dates, but I am not ready." I would rather wear wool underwear than have this conversation. "I think I am going to marry myself. My entire adult life, I have someone else to consider. Someone that needs to know where I am and when I am going to be home and what's for dinner.'"

"I would love to have to be responsible for someone else." I hadn't considered his position "I am going to be so nice to the next girl. I think of how badly I treated Jillian."

"Good. You should feel bad." The rain started in earnest and getting my phone wet. "Honey, it is pouring rain right now. I have to bust a move before I get too much wetter. I love you."

While working out in the weight room one Tuesday morning, I noticed a woman, through the window, doing Zumba. Bored out of my gourd, I was struggling to finish my workout. She looked like she was having a good time and was going to finish her workout with a smile on her face. I thought that maybe I could invite more joy into my life. My work out doesn't have to be dreary. There were enough dreary tasks in my days.

There was internal conflict when I started going to Zumba classes. My ego was taking a beating because I realized it was harder than it looked and I had to ask myself if I need to flounder in another part of my life. It was less like dancing and more like flailing about. The people who attend regularly know the steps and hand movements because the instructors do the same routines every week with little variance, which gave me hope. If I just kept going, it seemed that I might learn to dance even though it doesn't come natural. The high-octane music drowned out any gloomy thoughts, and the people were so nice in their guidance.

One hindrance was guilt. How could I be dancing when my son is suffering? It is said that a mother can only be as happy as her least happy child. Fortunately, my sense of justice kicked in; it didn't seem reasonable or fair to limit my life based on his refusal to get help for his disease. It didn't even seem to be helpful. It helped no one for me to trudge through life. I have preached the Buddhist expression to my kids: "Pain is inevitable and suffering is optional." Apparently, these were words just falling out of my mouth with no action.

Happiness wasn't going to arrive on my doorstep one day as a gift from someone who loves me when my life is perfect. I had to take responsibility. So, I went about my life injecting joy. I filled my hummingbird feeders and planted more flowers. I threw my ugly furniture away and all the clothing that might be practical but I didn't feel good wearing. I went more often to the movies and took more walks with friends. I committed to being happy even if my life wasn't ideal. I repeated the mantra over and over: "Happiness is not situational."

There were days that I was consumed by worry and didn't want to dance, but I forced myself. After several weeks at the back of the room, I moved to the front of the room so I could see the instructor better. I was nervous about the front row. The front row is for the students who know all the dances, so I stayed to the farthest left side of the front row. I worried that people would notice my struggle.

I recognized some of the songs from Claire's car radio but couldn't relate to moving to it. My arms and leg gestures were spastic. I couldn't figure out where this courage was coming from. When I invited a friend to come to class with me, she hit a sore spot by saying, "That's cheerleader stuff." When I was growing up, my dad's best friend's daughter, Gina, was a cheerleader. When he talked about her in glowing terms, I would burn with jealousy. In truth, my dad had never seen her cheer, but she always wore the latest fashions which I could not afford, and more importantly, she was confident which I also could not afford. I was so envious of her I couldn't even speak to her. The story I told myself is that she thought she was too good to talk to me. This might have been true except that I had beaten her to the punch by shrinking out of communication range.

I was going to four classes a week and slowly got more comfortable. Once I could figure out the moves, I was in step with the rest of the class, but the transitions were, as always, the problem. The idea that I could make a fool of myself in a room full of mostly women was fascinating. I also noticed that I talked to myself with ridicule when I made a misstep. Because I was doing something that has no impact to my income or relationships, I could be objective in my observation. I noticed how many other places in my life that I gave myself these messages. I couldn't even look in the mirror while I was dancing. I didn't even look at other people in the mirror because I might see myself. I followed the woman's steps next to me and told her what I was doing so she didn't think I was stalking her. She started helping me by indicating the next move, which kept me in time.

One day after a particularly hard class that involved holding small weights, a woman approached me, asking me, "Do you mind feedback from someone who has been doing this a hundred years?"

I told her of course, I would welcome feedback. She, with a straight face, asked me, "Do you hear the music?"

Without missing a beat, I told her, "Thank you for noticing that I am stretching myself and living on my growing edge." This therapy thing was working out for me. I didn't crumple in on myself or apologize for my existence or launch into a lengthy story explaining myself. This was astounding. I have apologized for my existence and my perceived inadequacies my entire life.

If I wanted Dylan to look in the metaphorical mirror, I had to learn to look in the mirror. Months into this experiment, I looked and saw a small fit woman with a giant smile and long gray hair staring back. I got a haircut the following day, but everything else was okay. My arm movements were still choppy, but my feet looked like they were dancing. Every time I looked, I was smiling because I love dancing. I had no idea that I had this in my wheelhouse. My Friday-night classes helped to ease the loneliness. As I was committed to only spending time with people who were not part of the fun house mirror, there was a vacuum in my social calendar. I didn't need to start the weekends with a pity party; I might as well dance.

Eventually, I looked like I was dancing instead of having a seizure. As I got happier, people were attracted to me and invited me places. There was collateral beauty as well; my backside looked the best it had ever looked. Much to Robbie and Claire's chagrin, I was dancing all the time, even to commercials. God help us all if one of my Zumba songs played in the grocery store. Sometimes, when someone in my home does something ridiculous, we ask, "Can you hear the music?"

"Hi, Dylan, how are you?" I spoke to him earlier in the day, and he sounded blue. "I was wondering what Plato and Socrates would say about the low voter turnout?" I wanted to be able to talk about the things that interested Dylan, so I started looking famous philosophers up on Wikipedia.

"I don't know, Mom." My attempt to distract him was translucent. "I don't feel good. I am really lonely."

"What about the other student's in your school?" There was silence on the other end. "I know you told me that they are either a lot younger or older than you and there are only eight people in a class, but do they participate in clubs? Like literary groups or creative writing circles."

The conversation went like this for forty-five min-utes—me pushing and pulling and his flat affect until both of us gave up trying. "I love you."

Finally

"Mom, I don't want you to get how you get." The direction this conversation was going meant that I might have to stop what I was doing. My stomach fluttered.

"Is this going to be a good conversation or a bad conversation?" I sighed, a long deep sigh to prepare for the worst. "Just say it."

"I started going to meetings, and I have been sober for three days." He could not see my tears, but he knows me too well. "Stop crying. This is why I didn't want to tell you. You always overreact, and I just don't want you to pressure me."

"I won't pressure you, but how many meetings are you going to?" Seriously, what is wrong with me? He just told me not to do this. "Okay, I'm sorry. How do you feel?"

"Physically, I feel better than I did. The first couple of days were hard. I had diarrhea and I was sweating. I guess I drink more than I realize." He could not see my ear-to-ear smile. "Don't get too excited. Mom, could you just stop?"

"What? I am not doing anything." I was standing on the corner, just letting cars have the right-of-way. "I am just excited for you."

"I talk to my sponsor every day. He's just a few years older than me, and he has a full-sleeve tattoo and has the cutest baby." I must have looked like a lunatic to the people driving by me. I was talking with my hands and inadvertently holding up traffic. They were waiting for me to cross, but I was waving them forward.

Dylan decided to get sober after Robert, one of his friends from rehab, overdosed and died. Dylan felt responsible for two reasons. Dylan had been the one who talked them into checking out of rehab by drinking. Dylan is usually the smallest in the group, but the most influential. Secondly, after none of them were granted forgiveness from the program, they all went their separate ways finding cars to sleep in or an overhang to keep the rain off if no car was available. Robert still kept in touch because Dylan was the only one with a car. Dylan had given Robert a ride to his dealer and then the hotel. Robert was ultimately found by the housekeeper. The fact that there were no services held for his friend or public acknowledgement bothered Dylan. He couldn't help seeing his own future.

Hearing the AA words coming out of his mouth was intoxicating. He had a sponsor and started working his steps. Two weeks into his sobriety, he was having trouble getting out of bed. He was lonely and overwhelmed. I made arrangements to visit him for four days by myself. I stayed in his room, which was remarkably clean. The courtyard men he shared the boarding home with looked exactly the way I imagined them to look like. They praised Dylan for being respectful and helpful.

I had heard the most about Chris and his wife, Ellen, because Dylan took them shopping once a week, and they bought him a six-pack for payment. Chris was over six feet and three hundred pounds; he was powerfully strong before his alcoholism slipped out of control and his knee gave up carrying the extra weight with no help from the rest of his body. His wife looked frightened and threadbare. She left a twenty-year abusive marriage to marry Chris who beat her up on their wedding night, and she missed work for three days afterward. He served in the Marines and was sure to remind Dale that the Marines garner more respect than the Army.

Dale served in the Army, and we know this because he wears an Army hat at all times, and the Army is the topic of conversation until interrupted. He was the only one that got up for work every day. He had been working for two years at the shipyard and hates sea lions because they are intrusive in his work. I flinched when he told me that sometimes he shoots them with the gun he carries everywhere. The gun is worrisome as he starts the morning with a shot of cheap rum in his coffee and continues in earnest after work. He told me that he considers Dylan to be his son because his relationship with his own kids is in tatters after a life of drinking and long stretches in unemployment with no child support.

Dale and Chris were jockeying for position with the other men that used the courtyard as a meeting area. Besides the men living in the building, there are others that gather to smoke and drink. Some looked homeless. I looked out of place because I am a woman and I was wearing clean clothes that are currently in fashion, even if they are eccentric. When they learned I was Dylan's mother, they told me about the favors and kindness that Dylan had done for them. He was respected by these people. I was proud that, even in his use, he is kind.

After doing his laundry and grocery shopping, we went to AA meetings and wandered around Astoria as tourists. When we walked in the meeting, Dylan shrunk beside me. Some of the people in the meeting knew him by name and were concerned that they had not seen him in a few days. He explained that he was getting ready for my visit. He refused to answer the question "Is there anybody in the first thirty days?" He was agitated that I elbowed him to encourage him to answer the question.

He walked out of the meeting during the final prayer in order to avoid further contact with the members. He was angry when we got in the car. "I am not going to speak in meetings, Mom."

Not knowing when to stop, I responded, "I think that the question is designed to solidify the first step." I continued even though his forehead was wrinkled and his lip quivered. "When we say I am so-and-so and I am an alcoholic, it's hard to unsay or, more importantly, unknow the fact that we are alcoholic." I stopped there and suggested we go kayaking.

Some of our best days as a family have been spent kayaking the Klamath River on the California and Oregon border. For years, it was a part of our family trips to Dunsmuir. We packed the Ford Explorer and put the racks on top with three kayaks. We borrowed or rented the rest of the boats. My favorite memory is the first time Dylan had his own boat with his friend since infancy, Didi. They were in a boat that was determined to be stable with a wide bottom, but it is more like rowing a bucket than a boat.

For ten miles, they rowed the bucket through class 2 and 3 rapids. At one point, they got too close to the trees along the banks. Both boys were terrified going under the low-hanging branches which threatened to knock them out of the boat. All I could do was yell instructions and watch them negotiate the bucket. They were screaming the Lord's Prayer as they were going under.

When the boat came out from under the trees, I saw only Dylan's head. My stomach dropped; Didi's mom, Linda, was going to have my head. She was nervous sending him with me to begin with. The last time she went camping with us, there was a baby rattlesnake in our campsite. She spent a great deal of time worrying about the mother rattlesnake. Camping was too dirty for her, so she stayed in a little hotel close to the campsite.

The only reason he was permitted to come with me was that she loved s'mores, and our kids were interchangeable in each other's home. One time, Linda even breastfed Claire while I was at work. Claire was inconsolable and cried for two hours until the nanny knocked on Linda's door. When I came home, she was lying on my bed, asleep with Claire tucked up under her arm.

I was relieved when Didi's dark hair popped out from the nose of the boat. He had tucked himself in the storage area in front. That evening, as they were changing in their small tent, I heard Dylan ask Didi, "Did you pee when we were going under?" Didi answered, "A little." They were applauding their abilities with the trees growing in size with every telling.

We went kayaking with hundreds of sea lions on a rare sunny day on the Columbia River and walked for miles on the pier. I had seen the photos that Dylan had taken of these places during his photography project, but photos can never fully capture the experience. I was happy he lived in such a beautiful place. Dylan had to take a nap afterward. He was taking Kratom supplement, which I thought was causing the nausea and headache.

The next day, we hung around bookstores and watched comedians on Netflix. We talked for hours about philosophy, which I know nothing about. School had invigorated brain cells he thought he had damaged. I hadn't seen the real Dylan in years. I wanted this to last forever and tried to extract promises of prolonged sobriety which, of course, he couldn't. One afternoon was tense as he pointed out, "Nothing is ever good enough for you." There were tears in his voice which made me stop.

"I know, you are right." I was truly sorry. "I am sorry."

"You want me to live into a standard that I don't want to live into." As I listened to him, I felt the tug of manipulation, but I rebuffed the notion that he was saying this so I would lower my standards. I couldn't figure out the next move, so I didn't reply.

As I stood in silence, I finally understood what it means to "stand as presence" like Doris had been teaching. For the remaining two days, I was with him in the now. There was no past, future, or expectation. I was able to enjoy his company and bookmarked these days in my heart. He reacted to this by staying calm during a scary incident involving a flat tire while we were driving.

Usually he would panic and start yelling, but he stayed focused on the solution. Finding tires in Astoria is impossible. We had to stop at every gas station and fill the tire in order to get to the next stop. His Ford Explorer was an older model, so tires were not abundant, and when we did find, the tires were cost prohibitive. All the tires, according to two tire technicians, were dangerous for the upcoming rains, so we needed to replace all four tires. I watched in awe as he handled himself with composure and humor. I was filled with hope; maybe this was the time he would make it in sobriety. I finally understood that I was taking his alcohol and drug abuse personally. It wasn't personal. It affects me, but he isn't doing this to me.

Now that I could hear him, he told me about his career decision. He was going to work toward being a high school teacher because he felt he had a lot of experience to offer the kids. It was a position of power in that he could change people's lives. He worried that he wasn't aiming high enough in his aspirations. Teachers don't make very much money.

I told him about my eleventh-grade teacher Mrs. Burney. Mrs. Burney wore berets every day because she was in treatment for ovarian cancer. She took me under her wing and arranged for me to be her teacher's aide. I took her English class and her speech class two years in a row. I was the captain of the debate team. She is the only reason that I graduated from high school. I agreed that being a teacher is a position of great power. The day I graduated, she gave me a beautiful pink umbrella with a wooden handle. The card that went with it contained words I have never heard before. She told me that I was "spectacular and should not accept anything but love."

My worry in high school was that people would find out that I was living in an insanely abusive household and had an abusive boyfriend. Her gift was not the umbrella even though it was the prettiest thing I had ever owned, but the reality that I was not invisible. If Dylan could give that to someone else, his life would be well spent.

Leaving was difficult. I missed my plane because we were talking and forgot to pay attention to the time, and I almost missed the second plane still talking. I didn't know if I would ever be with him like this again. I was crying when I boarded. The woman sitting next to me was a mom of five adult children whose husband just left her for a younger, skinnier version of herself. The flight was only an hour and fifteen minutes, but I learned her whole history.

He stayed sober another week and started drinking, occasionally claiming that the people in AA are hypocritical and, my favorite, "AA is a cult." Disappointment is composed of hope and failure. It might be better to never have the hope if it is not going to materialize into success. I started counting the attempts. It takes, on average, seven attempts at sobriety before it sticks. We were on attempt three; my prayer is that he lives through the rest of the attempts.

I have since been able to stand in presence on occasion; even while he is so intoxicated, he can't speak intelligently. There are moments absent of fear or anger and only love exists. These moments foster trust and respect. I am not a saint, though, so the moments are far and few between, but they continue to be my goal.

"Hi, Dylan." I called to talk about the new Bill Burr comedy special on Netflix.

"Did you see the new Bill Burr special?" he asked me before I could ask him. I laughed and explained that I was calling to ask him if he had seen it yet.

"I was wondering if you are managing your drinking to just the few beers a night." I was treading lightly.

"I think I am doing okay with it. Maybe I am one of those people they talk about in the big book that drink heavy for a while and then become normal drinkers." He sounded confident.

"Maybe. Just keep an eye on it." We talked for thirty minutes before hanging up.

Dead Cat Syndrome

"Hi, honey. It's so early. What are you doing up so early on a Saturday morning?" I was trying to find my shoe under the bed. "Are you okay? I can't talk long. I am going to breakfast with Jennifer."

"I am okay. Are you dating her?" Crap, this might be this way forever. Every friend is going to be suspect. "No. Jennifer is happily married to a man."

"I am not dating, so chill. I need another partner like I need a hole in my head." My irritation was audible.

"Why did you tell us you are gay if you are not going to date?" Despite being a reasonable question, I was defensive in my reply.

"I thought it would take pressure off Dad because there is a reason for the separation, and he doesn't have to defend himself to others, and it felt like it is more fair to the next partner I have if they are not meeting a new relationship with the shock of my sexual orientation." This was my practiced response, but I hated saying it. I hated talking about it.

He must have hated it too because his response was just as irritable. "Ewww. Don't say sexual orientation."

Now I was having fun with his discomfort with my standard sex talk with my kids. "Don't worry, I have only had sex three times. Just enough to make three babies. I gotta go, though, because I am late." I hung up still irritated.

As I was getting in her car, I looked down the driveway in our condo complex and saw a dead cat. Dear Reader, I am aware that this is a bad-mother moment. I went back into the house and woke up Claire to go look at the cat and determine if it was my cat or the neighbor's cat. The reason this was not my finest parenting moment is that Claire loves her two cats more than she likes most people. I just didn't have the fortitude to look at my dead cat before breakfast. It had been a chaotic week.

I watched as she approached the cat, still wearing her pajamas. My stomach was in a knot as I wondered if I was going to have to cancel the breakfast to deal with the body. Would I be an ogre if I threw the body away and went to breakfast? I had been looking forward to the breakfast and AA meeting, and it wouldn't benefit anyone if I stayed home. The optics would be terrible, but the cat wouldn't be any more alive if I sat home. I was confused when Claire started laughing hysterically.

It wasn't a cat at all. It was a branch with leaves. I was conflicted by relief that I didn't have to deal with a dead cat and mortified that I saw a dead cat that was really a branch. The universe was talking again. I wondered how many dead cats were in my life. How many times did I look at events through the lens of fear or desire? I think I suffer from dead cat syndrome. My perception is affected by my deep fears or wants, but the most powerful mixture is when I have deep fear and a want at the same time.

The stories I tell myself distort my reality. I am not alone in this condition however. Once I acknowledged this truth, I saw it in other people in real time. It took several weeks in Josh's office of pushing and pulling on the whys and hows of my behavior to move closer to the truth. Like a bull terrier with a chew toy, we kept circling around this issue because, according to Josh, the truth is sacred. The work in his office is to get as close to the truth as possible. It is removing the fun house mirrors so that I can realize my potential.

Years ago, I heard a TV psychologist say, "Humans only do behavior that works for them on some level." I can't remember the show or person who said it, but I remember the audience member who was pushing back on this statement. She was a woman my age in a bad marriage who had been victimized several times in her life. The doctor asked her why she thinks she chose an abusive man after having been abused her whole life.

She responded with the obvious, "This is what I am used to."

He was physically in her space with the microphone almost touching her lips. There was no escaping him, and he was experienced. This was not going to end well; her reality was about to be shattered. Her lip quivered with his follow-up question, "How is this working for you?"

The tears spilled over their brim and down her cheeks as she told him her lengthy tale of abuse and suffering, ending in, "This was not my fault."

"Somehow, these choices have worked for you on some level." He did not care that she was sobbing; he pressed on,

"As painful as your choices are, your options are perceived to be more painful."

She was leaning on him for stability. "You give away your power because you don't believe that you are capable of making your own decisions. This way you can always blame someone else." I was angry while I listened. "You are abdicating your responsibility."

I was so angry sitting on my bed, holding my socks in my hands. I was already late to my appointment. Who was this guy to be blaming the victim? Has he ever heard of the term *victim blaming*? Then he told the story of escaping an abusive childhood and his drug addiction. His life changed once he understood the payoff for victimhood. He acknowledged that he had no power when he was a child to change his circumstance, but in adulthood, he was still acting powerless because he always had a *because*. I lost my job *because* I am homeless *because* ad infinitum. It never ends.

At this point, I had to put my running shoes on because I was going to be late for my appointment even if I ran. I wasn't going to miss his next statement, "People can't take power. You give them power. The cost to keep your power might persuade you to give your power away, but it's important to understand that you have the power initially. We are in a cost-benefit analysis at all times." And finally, "Sometimes we overestimate the cost."

I was useless at the appointment after getting there too late to be helpful, and I could barely form a sentence. What if I had been wrong? What if I overestimate the cost of taking responsibility in my life? What would I do differently?

What is the actual cost? Could I trust my ability to deal with the truth? I didn't know what to do with this new reality but to bookmark it for later reference. Sitting in the car on my way to breakfast, this truth was in my face again.

As long as I see myself as a victim in Dylan's life, he has the power. When Dylan wants me to see things his way, he just has to talk nice to me because I am afraid of rejection. He knows this tender part of my psyche and uses it to his advantage by painting a picture for me that is most appealing. I am so easily manipulated by my own fears and desires. The more intense the want, the easier it for someone to shift the power away from me.

This vulnerability is not limited to family; anyone can use my fear against me. Customers used if for years, telling me that if I didn't give them the answers they wanted in their appraisal reports, they would simply use another appraiser and not pay for the report. I wasn't the only appraiser that was being abused in this way as evidenced during the market crash. I know four appraisers in my market that lost their licenses because of fraudulent reports. I was more afraid of the governing board, so I didn't push the values, but I compensated for this by working seven days a week to have the fastest turn times in the market. I hadn't had a vacation in eleven years.

The Wednesday before Thanksgiving, the power company called me with a notice that my power was going to be disconnected within fifteen minutes unless I could give them a cash payment of $498.25. Intellectually, I knew that I had recently made a payment but wondered if they didn't process the payment. I was also aware that their demand was unreasonable and not likely to be legal, but they had clarified by saying that it was a red flag account because I had previous disconnections. My gut was telling me that this was fraud, but my fear of being disconnected and unable to reconnect until the following day, which was Thanksgiving moved me forward to co-operate with the instructions.

The man, David King, kept calling me to see where I was in the process so he could delay the disconnection time. I thanked him several times for helping me. It wasn't until they called the next day, looking for another payment, and Claire was in the room did I realize that I had been conned. I felt stupid. I couldn't believe that I had let my fear override reason. Their attention to detail was impressive. The phone number was the right area code, and they had used the phone tree options from the power company. They even transferred me to the manager when I asked to talk to the supervisor. When I was on the phone, I had a stirring in my gut that told me I was being robbed, and I even suggested this when they told me that if I didn't pay the full amount, I would be out of power for the weekend because they would be closed for the weekend. I know the power company doesn't act in such a careless way, but the fear was dictating my actions.

Every time I have been swindled, I ignored my gut reaction and let fear and panic prevail. I am even more pliable when it is my son. I had received a call at 2:00 a.m., asking for $40 for a cab because his car was going to be towed. Part of the payment is to help him because I love him and don't want to see him suffer, but part of the payment is to protect my future self. Just in case he is telling the truth. If something happened to him and I had the ability to help him with $40, I would be forever guilty.

Depending on the lens I am using for the day, I could see myself as foolish or determined. If I am feeling sorry for myself, I think I am a fool for believing him when he tells me ridiculous stories to get more money from me. If I am being compassionate with myself, I see myself as hopeful and loving. It's possible that both are true.

This ridiculous mistake should have just been an embarrassing event before breakfast with my friend, but I had surrounded myself with a support team of friends, a good therapist, and family that kept pushing on my truths, asking the question, "Is that true?"

"Did you have a good breakfast?" His voice was slurred because it was after five o'clock.

"Yes. Did you have a good day?" I was getting used to dealing with him in his current state. "It's nice to have a friend. I haven't had a friend like this in years. She likes being with me and doesn't want anything from me but to be her friend."

"That's what I want." I wanted that for him too, but I know that I never had friends like this when I was drinking and using drugs.

"You will when you get sober." Why did I have to say this? What is wrong with me that I can't leave well enough alone?

"Yep. I have to go now." He closed up and hung up.

What Am I Seeing?

"I met a girl." Dylan was happier than I had heard him in a long time. "She's so good, Mom."

"What's her name, and where did you meet her?" This was good news. Maybe it would help his depression.

"Her name is Emily, and I met her at school. We get along so good. She has Asperger's syndrome, so she is socially awkward, but she is so nice." He was tripping over his words. "We spent all day yesterday together. That's why you couldn't get ahold of me."

"Have you met her family? Are they nice? Does she drink a lot?" I knew my mom questions would bug him, but I might get away with it this time.

"I met her family and used my best manners. They like me. Her mom made us dinner, and no, Emily does not drink a lot. In fact, she hardly drinks at all." I was running late to a doctor's appointment, so I couldn't talk long.

"When can I meet her?" I thought this was going to be annoying, but he was eager for us to meet each other.

"She wants to meet you too because I talk a lot about you." I hung up with a smile on my face and an amen.

I was happy for him and continued to support him in his studies both economically and emotionally. This was what I always wanted for him. They were doing homework together and spending all their time together. She didn't have a job and only taking two classes, so there was a lot of dead time. They slept a lot, and Dylan started missing classes.

He regularly tamped down my fears by explaining he was in a new relationship and his grades were holding steady. His speech was slurred more frequently, and he needed more money. I knew that I should investigate further, so I flew them both down to my home for a visit. Emily was nervous to meet me, but I was excited.

They flew in on a Thursday in May. They both looked shabby and exhausted. They fell asleep before dinner and then stayed up all night, eating candy. I had told them before they came that I would be happy to spend a few hundred dollars apiece on new clothing because they were both wearing threadbare clothing. I also told them that they could use marijuana, but I didn't want drinking in the home. His behavior is tolerable on marijuana; too much made him sleep. No harm no foul. Drinking was a no-holds-barred game. He was so angry with this boundary that he cancelled the trip until Emily begged him to make the trip.

Emily was nice but never smiled even while shopping for the clothing she wanted. The clothing she was wearing had holes that she didn't seem to notice. Her face and arms had scabs where she had picked her skin. She wouldn't wear short sleeves. It was ninety-eight degrees, and everyone else in my house was wearing shorts and tank tops as my air conditioner is weak, but they were both in long sleeves.

The second day, they stayed in bed all day in my living room.

We were supposed to go to San Francisco's Fisherman's Wharf and Pier 39, but I couldn't even get them out of bed to play a game of cards or eat at the table with the rest of us. I thought they were sick and offered them at least one hundred cups of tea. They seemed to know each other well, but they didn't seem to like each other. There were no tender moments that I would expect in a new relationship. They did get out of bed to go to the smoke shop and bought Kratom, the herbal supplement. They took several at a time.

Panic ran from my stomach through the top of my head when I saw his filthy white T-shirt after he finally removed his sweater. Dylan had inherited my vanity, and this would never be acceptable if he was healthy. Emily was confused when I started crying over a T-shirt, but Dylan understood. He started yelling at me that I was overreacting and that he was just depressed. I walked to Target that day and bought him new white T-shirts, socks, and underwear. This trip was going so differently than I had imagined. I thought we would be going to the Ashby flea market the day after we went to San Francisco. I was prepared to pay a ridiculous amount of money on dinner in San Francisco. The futon in the living room was their home base, and candy wrappers and soda cans were scattered about the tables, flooring, and the end of the bed and the bed frame.

I confronted them the morning of their flight and told them that they needed to know that they looked strung out. They looked down at their hands while Dylan explained they were just tired, and I was paranoid. I pointed out that they were nineteen and twenty-two years old and it's not possible for healthy young adults to be this exhausted unless chemicals are involved or they have cancer. Dylan railed against me, pointing out that if I had let them drink alcohol, their trip would have been better. I was treating him like a child, and he didn't feel it was necessary to engage with someone who didn't recognize him as an adult.

It was my hope that I was wrong and he was right. We made peace before he flew back to Oregon to finish his semester. I hugged Emily goodbye and implored her to take care of my son. My whole effort in this trip was to align with her in my effort to curb his substance abuse. I knew that his life would be better if he just put the substances in their place. After all these experiences, I still didn't know if he needed to be entirely sober. Maybe he was one of the users that could drink normally after a time of abuse. That wasn't my experience, but I have met people that have had this experience. I made it my practice in sobriety to let others decide if they are alcoholic or drug addicts.

"Hi, honey." I tried to control the relief in my voice. "I have been calling you to say how nice it was to meet Emily."

"Sorry, I haven't been ignoring you." I wish I hadn't called every waking hour for the last two days. "I was studying for finals."

"That's okay. I knew you were good." I sounded crazy. I knew that he could see the call history. "I hope you are taking care of yourself." We talked for another thirty minutes before hanging up with I love yous.

Just Punch Me in the Face

I continued calling Dylan every day just to chat or check in on his health and well-being. He answered occasionally at odd hours. His expenses were rising as he was carrying the financial weight of the relationship. His speech was garbled while he was asking for more money for photography project materials. There were more emergencies popping up, doctor bills that needed to be paid before they would see him again, money that needed to be paid back on loans used for groceries and more chaos. I supported all these expenses but speculated that I was being manipulated.

The business was clipping along at a steady pace, but we weren't swimming in money. If I was giving him money, there was another responsibility that wasn't met. I was happy to get him through the semester and proud that I had two kids in college. This is what I always wanted. I would tell anybody who was willing to listen that I had two kids in college. This time in our history was designed to be a life reset. It felt like I was making up for any mistakes I had made in my decision-making. If I had been wrong when I sent him to the therapeutic boarding school, this would make up for lost education.

He blamed me for his life choices because he was rejected when I sent him away. I was still ambivalent after all these years. He was hitting a soft spot for me because I had been rejected as a child. I reminded myself during these moments of doubt that I wrote to him every day and gave him every chance to turn his behavior around. We would have been evicted from our rental if we were to have the volatile interactions with screaming and violence that end in police intervention. We are all in the same boat, and no one has the right to poke holes in the boat.

Before our move to the condo, our neighbors were so eager to see us move from my dream home they helped us load the truck. They would not have to listen to the early-morning screaming matches in the converted garage office. The garage was not well insulated, and they could hear every profanity-laced tirade. There were days that I stayed indoors all day after particularly explosive events. Maybe the move would be a fresh start with new neighbors who didn't know that we were lunatics.

He took his finals on a Tuesday, and on Wednesday, his car was wrecked by a friend in a hit-and-run. He let a guy with an expired driver's license drive his SUV to move out of the building that Dylan was living in. Dylan was in the car when the guy fell asleep and hit a parked car. Dylan got out of the car to leave his information with the car's owner when the sleepy driver grabbed Dylan's five-feet, four-inch body and pulled him back in the car to drive away. Dylan was in a quagmire. He was scared of this middle-aged man who was twice his size and even more scared of the police. His car was broken down on a side street. When they separated; Dylan called the police.

"Mom, I am sorry." He was calling from Emily's home. "I need you to stop yelling at me."

"I am sorry too." I was glad he finally called. "Thank you for letting me be a part of your life, even in the muck."

He told me about the police interaction. The police officer, a man under the age of thirty, congratulated him for doing the right thing while taking the report. I became furious and suspicious when he asked for help repairing the car. While I was relieved that he was alive, I was angry with the circumstance. I couldn't understand why Dylan wasn't driving, and I couldn't understand how it's possible to fall asleep driving five miles across town. I couldn't understand why he was so careless with the car we had given him. I was screaming at him for being irresponsible with the car that we pay for and insure. He was hurt that I wasn't being more supportive. He was scared and shaking, and I was distraught. There were lame excuses coming back at me. He was terrified of retribution as the guy had a warrant for his arrest.

He needed a place to hide because the guy's friends already warned Dylan that he had a target on his back. He swore up one side and down another that he would never lend his car again. The repairs cost a total of $800, which Craig and I split. He eventually came out of hiding, and then there was another emergency call in the middle of the night.

"Mom." His voice was filled with panic. "I need $40 for a cab to get my car in Seaside before it's towed."

I was confused when he called, thinking I was dreaming. We already had this conversation. He had already gotten $40 in the middle of the night. I hung up the phone, thinking I had made a mistake.

He was angry when he called back. "Why did you hang up on me?"

"You already used this excuse." I was half awake. "You are going to have to be more creative."

He explained that he was being nice to a girl who needed help. Summer, a pretty girl he spoke of often, had borrowed his car three days prior and abandoned the car in a parking lot fifteen miles away. Again, Dylan was forced to bring the police into his situation. They found his car, but the car was going to be towed if he didn't get to the car within one hour, and the cab cost $40, and of course, he would need money for gas. I sent the money to him and then tried to go back to sleep, but there was no sleep. I didn't hear from him for two days after the crisis.

I was out with friends the next day but didn't mention the midnight crisis because I was embarrassed by my problem. My friends were professional women higher up on the Maslow's hierarchy of needs. They weren't worried about giving their grocery money to fix their son's car. I limited my use of Dylan's name during the day. I had grown tired of the sound of my own voice. The look on people's faces when I spoke the specifics of the situation was compassion mixed with pity. I needed their friendship, so I learned to be vague and move on to happier topics of conversation.

After a few days of Dylan having to be in hiding again because he had, again, called the police on someone with a warrant, he finally called. I was so grateful that he called that it didn't bother me that it was one in the morning. I asked him where he had met Summer, and without thinking, he replied, "At the needle exchange." I wasn't sure I heard it correctly, but my body heard it. I sat on the floor hard and looked for something to vomit into. I saw the truth in sharp focus. There were dead cats everywhere.

"I am going to kill Lucy." Claire's cat. "She peed in the corner near my yoga mat."

"Mom, did you hear me?" This time, it was his turn to be confused.

"Yes, I heard you. I don't know what I am supposed to say right this second." This is not what I planned for my night. "Is it heroin?"

"Yes. I wanted to tell you a hundred times. I hinted at it so many times I thought you knew." The relief in his voice was clear.

"I guess a part of me knew, but the other part of me didn't want me to know. My brain is so weird. It can purposefully not see the truth." I could hear my voice, but it wasn't me talking.

Was he using dirty needles? Not anymore. I knew instantly that I had been buying his heroin. Not only his drugs but his girlfriend's too. How could I be so blind? The truth was staring me in the face, and I ignored the facts, telling myself a story. Even when I visited him in September, he was using Kratom, which is an herbal opioid used to detox. He was popping them like candy at my house. In fact, he was sick when he was visiting me. He was dope sick. I was offering him tea like an idiot. I was literally killing him with my love.

I didn't tell anyone for several days. I was hollowed out as if someone had scooped out my organs while I wasn't looking. I asked Robbie and Claire if they knew. Robbie knew when he had made Dylan pull up his sleeves during his visit. There were track marks on both arms. The first time I spoke the truth was in a Saturday morning women's AA meeting. The words *my son is a heroin addict* tasted foul in my mouth. There was only one way out of this; I was going to have to be truthful.

Potentially, part of the drug problem in the over-all community is the shame of the family. When I talked about my children with other mothers, I would tell them about Claire and Robbie. Then I would mention that my son was suffering from a heroin addiction. The statements were factual in nature and meant to be brief, but frequently, the mothers would admit they also had children who were addicts. I was shattering the illusion of the suburban family. We were supposed to be productive and happy, not trying to find the nearest methadone clinics.

There was no contact with Dylan for two days after this conversation. I was moving through my life distracted with worry. I couldn't properly hear people talking to me, only grabbing a few words at a time. My responses didn't make any sense. It was a lot of effort being in public. I was missing sleep regularly. I tried to only call Dylan twice a day. It took a monk's discipline to keep from calling every ten minutes. One morning, I woke up with my phone in my hand. The call history showed that I had called Dylan twenty-one times in the night. I had given my power away again. He was going to use this to his advantage. My worry was his best manipulation tool. After that night, I put my phone in another room so that I would be able to stay disciplined even when my defenses were weak in the night.

I finally heard from Dylan, who told me that Summer had come to his door and offered him a hit in a conciliatory effort. It was a hotshot designed to overdose him. Dylan took the hit and slept for four hours. When he woke up, Summer was still in the room with him and told him, "Don't ever call the police on someone again" and left. It occurred to me that he was being cruel telling me this. I didn't know what to do with the information. It was possible that he needed someone to know what happened, and I was the only one still talking to him. I had to go out into the world though with this new reality and act normal.

Walking around the grocery store, I noticed people having mundane conversations about pasta sauce and was consumed with envy. I had to figure out my next step. Dylan had declared he was going to stop using drugs. He would only drink a couple beers in the evening. I couldn't support him anymore. I paid the last-month rent but stopped sending money.

"Mom, I am going to be homeless again." He was making a last-ditch effort.

"This is killing me." I was sobbing. "I don't know what to do. I have tried everything to help you, but all I seem to be doing is killing you. This is, by the far, the hardest thing I have ever done." I had to hang up because I couldn't talk anymore. I took a shower at three in the afternoon and cried until the hot water ran cold.

On Target

"Hi, Dylan. Do you think I can see you today?" Part of me was relieved that I did not see him yet. Robbie, Claire and I had not yet fully unpacked our hiking gear from our trip up Mount Shasta. I didn't know if I had the stomach to see him dope sick.

"Dad and I are on our way over." I stopped working and was pouring tea and arranging chocolate chip cookies on a plate when they walked in.

Craig thought that seeing Dylan right away would be too difficult for me; Dylan had been at Craig's house for five days already. It took two days for them to come home from Oregon. Dylan couldn't be in the car for the entire trip as a whole. When Craig picked him up, his face had sores from picking his skin, he was pale, malnourished, and was vomiting with profound diarrhea. He gained eight pounds in a week but was still a shell of my son when I finally saw him. He was cranky and sensitive with no frustration tolerance. He spent a lot of time in my home but spent most of his time at Craig's home because Craig is more patient than I am.

One afternoon, Dylan came in while I was working at my desk, sat on the couch next to me, and confessed his sins. I wasn't looking at him, and he was looking straight ahead. He told me that he started doing heroin when a friend he admired from rehab stayed in his room and pressured him. He said he thought it would be just a weekend fling with the drug and he would go back to school with a new adventure under his belt. When he left, because Dylan is only allowed to have a guest for two nights, the guy stole the $300 camera we bought him for Christmas.

Apparently, it was love at first use. When Emily wanted to stop, Dylan didn't. When Dylan wanted to stop, Emily didn't. I asked him what about the high was worth giving up his whole life. His logic was clear and reasonable unless you consider reality. He said that when he looked at his empty life, it seemed foolish to deny himself pleasure today for tomorrow's benefit.

"It's like falling in love over and over." The wistful look he had on his face was contradictory with the healing sores.

"What do you want to do?" I tried not to plead. "Have you thought about rehab? I know you can't go to the same rehab as Emily, but we could find you one around here."

"I don't want to go to rehab." And with that, he went on with his confession and the reasons for his circumstance.

He recalled all the times his family had rejected him, specifically his being sent to rehab at fifteen years old. He took no responsibility for his actions. It was his opinion that his behavior was normal for a teenager. This was a sore spot for me because I wondered if I had been more patient would he have straightened up. As I was thinking about this, I looked across the room and noticed the black mark and chipping paint on the wall where the wall meets the ceiling.

It was from an incident after he had come home from the boarding school. He was angry with his father and me and threw a metal air soft gun across the room at Craig's head. He missed. That particular argument was about his painting the orange tip that identifies the gun as a toy. He painted it black, the same color as the rest of the gun. He wanted to go out with Robbie playing air soft. I thought my concern was obviously reasonable, but logic doesn't always matter. This was an argument worth having; I could lose two children with a simple misunderstanding with a well-meaning police officer.

His anger explodes in two ways. The most dangerous is the slow build because he can conserve the energy while stoking the fire. I frequently danced the dance with him in an effort to say something that will sink in later on; people don't always hear things the first time around. My energy feeds the anger, and the longer the argument, the more opportunity to say hurtful things that can't be unheard. The second kind of explosion is usually sudden and confusing. One hilarious explosion involved mashed potatoes in the microwave.

I microwaved mashed potatoes to reheat them after the turkey was carved and the gravy was ready for the table. Thanksgiving is a hard dinner to make, and you practically have to redecorate afterward because there is turkey fat coating the handles of the drawers. The mashed potatoes almost dropped out of my hands when Dylan yelled at me.

"Why did you microwave the potatoes? That ruins the texture, and the microwave is not good for you!" I nearly jumped out of my skin. "This is my favorite meal and you ruined it."

"What? You're a cocaine addict talking about the microwave being bad for you. That's rich." Thank God, it landed well, and after everyone sufficiently giggled at the absurdity, Dylan said grace.

I didn't argue about whose fault his situation is because being right was not the point. As long as he can't see his part, he can't change his circumstance.

His confession continued with stories of using dirty needles until he discovered the needle exchange, and then he presented me with a palm-sized device. When I asked him what it was, he explained that it is Narcan shot in case he overdoses.

"You know, Mom, you could accidently overdose on your medication too." I was startled to learn that he was drawing a false equivalency between my low dose of medication taken as directed and his shooting heroin in his arm. It would seem impossible to startle me anymore, but he has endless potential to teach me.

"Sorry, what?" I wanted him to say it again in case I misunderstood.

"We are addicted to the same thing, Mom." A few days ago, I was relieved to know he was alive, and with a flip of a switch, I was so angry I never wanted to see him again.

"No, we are not. I take pain medication as directed under a doctor's care. They are so careful with me because they know I am an addict. I have never once abused my medication!" I was screaming at him. I forgot I could get that mad.

As if I said nothing, he stated that I should keep the Narcan somewhere easy to find because it has to be used right away. I took it and put it on my desk, not wanting to touch it. My silence bothered him, and he asked me why I would be opposed to having it in my home. I took another minute to compose myself before I responded.

When I looked at the little canister, I flashed back to being up all night, watching his breathing, and the time that I looked over at him with his lips turning blue while sitting in the big bucket chair I kept in my room. I reminded myself that I was in the room when it happened—twice. This was a job that I wasn't qualified to do. It isn't for a lack of love but a lack of control of his actions. As much as I wanted to rule the world, it wasn't my turn. With all the love in my heart, I told him I would not keep it here in my home. I couldn't be responsible for his drug use. He was going to have to keep himself alive.

What I didn't say is that I didn't want to be the woman in Al-Anon that carries a Narcan in her pocket at all times in case her forty-three-year-old son living in her home overdoses. She cannot retire because she has spent her savings on him. Her life had been a fruitless sacrifice. Dylan took my refusal personally, taking it as another rejection.

"I am misleading you in my efforts to save you. I am telling you that I can save you, but I cannot. You have all the tools you need to recover your life. You have no felonies and you still have your health." I was preaching without shame. "Right now, if you cleaned up, it could be no harm no foul and you go about your merry way."

We spent several hours talking about his future and the attributes he offers the world. I reiterated that he is funny, loving, and intelligent and he is muting these characteristics with his drug and alcohol abuse. I offered one more time to help him get into rehab, but he didn't want to get sober. He wanted to stay off drugs, but he still wanted to drink alcohol. Emily's rehab in Oregon had run its course, and she was going to be released in a week. Dylan wanted to pick her up from rehab. Part of his motivation included her prescription for Suboxone, which is a synthetic opioid used to keep the user from using heroin. It prevents the user from getting high on the real stuff. Too much Suboxone gives a high similar to heroin.

I learned in our conversation that Justin had been sharing his Suboxone, and when he went back to Pennsylvania, he took his medicine with him. I had been praying for Justin to leave, but what I didn't know is that Dylan was addicted to the Suboxone and moved to the cheaper version—heroin. The fact that he was choosing the homeless option speaks of the power of the drug and not his intelligence. I had to keep chanting this over and over instead of the other version, "He is a freaking moron. What is wrong with him?"

In a moment of unadulterated bravery, I asked him, "What did I do that caused this? Did I make this happen?"

I braced for the truth. Would he remember that I read the entire *Harry Potter* series to him? Or would he remember that I grabbed him in a moment of anger when he rejected my spaghetti sauce? I thought when I had kids that they would love my cooking and talk about it with their kids, but in fact, he didn't like my cooking and often rejected it with great fanfare. Would he remember the walks to 7-Eleven to get a Slurpee, or would he prefer to dwell on the fact that I forgot him several times on early day Wednesdays, sometimes he could wait an hour?

Did he even know that Craig and I went to a child development class when I was pregnant with him, not a Saturday-morning three-hour class; we took a three-unit college credit class at the community college. We did homework. Okay, I did homework and some of Craig's. I don't recall the class talking about when your teenager overdoses or chooses to be homeless. We were coloring outside the lines at this point. Did he know how much I love him?

There was too much time before the answer, and I regretted asking. Potentially, he was being compassionate. "You made me take piano lessons."

My shoulder's loosened, and I laughed, relieved. "Oh, good. I thought it was my fault." I am never going to ask that question again.

The following day, I took him to Target. I bought him everything he would need to be homeless. We started with groceries, such as sandwich supplies, cereal, and snacks with high doses of sugar. We moved to the camp gear, such as a lantern with a ten-year battery and a headlamp to use while taking a leak in the night. Lots of toilet paper and baby wipes. Dry shampoo, shaving cream, and razors. Then we moved to the towels, blankets, interview shirts, and pants. Unfortunately or fortunately, I had experienced being homeless.

While I was packing the cart to check out, I appreciated the value of my experience. It was a humiliating experience, which still affects my self-esteem. It bothers me that I had been so fragile that I could not hold a job or put a roof over my head. I worried that I could be in this state again. All I had to do was pick up the first drink. The ugly gift of the experience is that I can't judge people. I have no right. People find me approachable, and I get to hear people's deepest, darkest secrets.

He spent the last night at my house, and we watched our favorite comedian, Louis C.K., and ate Chinese food. We talked about politics and laughed at old episodes of *The Office*. He had a hard time leaving but had to hurry to pick up Emily. I hugged him a long time and reminded him that he is very loved and he is strong. He can do this. I was practicing my cheerleading.

Broken Stories

Staying in my own lane took unknown discipline. I only called once a day, and if he didn't answer, I didn't call again. There were many dramas during his homelessness. Drunken arguments with Emily were regular events, peppered by money dramas. One morning, I received a call asking for money to professionally clean his car. During an argument three days prior, they had spilled or thrown milkshakes at each other, and now the car, already overstuffed, smelled like sour milk. He screamed profanity at me after I refused to send him money. I wanted to bring him home and fit him into my story of his life. He could go to college, meet a nice girl that he hasn't shared a needle with, and have babies.

The awareness of the stories in my own life steadied my resolve. My whole life was based on stories I inherited or absorbed. The stories dictated my role as a woman, wife, and mother. I was supposed to be a saint, always forgiving and ready to serve. As much as I wanted to stay plugged into people I personally barely know, with Facebook, I avoided the temptation. It's almost impossible for me to stop comparing my insides to other people's outsides. My mind tells me that these happy moments posted for the world to see are not representative of their every moment.

My value had been based on the value others assigned to me. It is ironic that I have worked so long as an appraiser—finding value. At fifty years old, I was breaking my stories. My life had changed radically by allowing myself to be content with reality. The ingredients had remained the same. I still lived in the same house, went to the same church, and ran the same business, but I participate more freely because I am choosing them. I chose joy more often, and I take every chance I have to dance.

I received a text from Dylan a few days after he had found a home. He and Emily were both working. The text was a YouTube video of Merle Haggard singing the song "Momma Tried." I was grateful that he recognized my efforts, but he has his own story to live. I only call when I want to hear his voice, and I only give what I want to give. It is easier to love when I am not judging my worth on his behavior. I wish that I could have learned this lesson earlier, and if I didn't love Dylan as much as I love him, I might not have ever learned the lesson.

Dear Reader, I told you that it would be a happy ending. I don't know the end of Dylan's story yet; he is still struggling with his addiction, and $20 could still kill him. In fact, the most respectful thing I could do is to trust the process. He has the tools, and it's my job to stay out of his way. My happy ending has to be good enough.

I became the person I was asking him to become.

About the Author

J. Marie, a native Californian, lives in the Bay Area where she raised her three children. She is active in the community with social justice work while running a small business.

CPSIA information can be obtained
at www.ICGtesting.com
Printed in the USA
BVHW071312260421
605863BV00003B/355